I0078709

ABCs of HEALING

Teaching Your Kids to Heal

by

Stephanie Middleton

COPYRIGHT INFO

© Copyright 2017 – Stephanie Middleton

All rights reserved. This book is protected by the copyright laws of the United States of America. This book may not be copied or reprinted for commercial gain or profit. The use of short quotations or occasional page copying for personal or group study is permitted and encouraged. Permission will be granted upon request. Scripture quotations are taken from the New King James Version. Copyright © 1979, 1980, 1982 by Thomas Nelson, Inc. Used by permission. All rights reserved. All emphasis within Scripture quotations is the author's own. The Strongest NASB Exhaustive Concordance. Copyright © 1981, 1998 by The Lockman Foundation. Used by Permission. All rights reserved. Please note that some of the children's names mentioned in this book have been changed to protect their privacy.

ISBN-13: 978-0-692-95528-4
ISBN-10: 0-692-95528-3

For Worldwide Distribution. Printed in the U.S.A.

"Behold, I and the children whom the Lord has given me are for signs and wonders in Mt. Zion."

Isaiah 8:18

DEDICATED TO

Our Children,
Noah, Tyler, Cailyn and Emma,

May your innocence, love, excitement, expectancy
and fearlessness richly bless you
and move hearts for more of Him.
May testimonies of your adventures with Daddy God
continue to increase, encouraging one another
until the glory of the Lord fills the earth.
May you grow in ever-increasing knowledge of Him,
embracing your childlikeness all the days of your life
as you search out His marvelous mysteries.
May you walk in all of His ways and always be aware
of His Presence with you wherever you go.

Love you always ~ Mom and Dad

IN HONOR OF

In honor of our Heavenly Dad and
my parents, Greg and Jane Moore, of Believing Jesus
Ministries; who pioneer with great faith into the miraculous,
pulling the body of Christ into their success.

Dad and Mom,
You are true coaches and cheerleaders of the faith.
Your love knows no bounds and we are so thankful
to learn and mature in faith through you; cultivating those
same principles in the lives of our children.
May we nurture and celebrate a fearless generation
of world changers in the love and power
of our Lord and Savior! Hallelujah!

OUR HOPE

To every person who is partnering
with Daddy God to bring Heaven to earth,

May you know Him intimately all the days of your life.
May you gladly give it a go, delighting in
the goodness of Daddy God's faithfulness.
May you continue to feed on the testimonies
of what God has done, is doing and will do!
May you dream bigger than what seems reasonable
and be amazed at Daddy God's ability to
far exceed your own expectations.
May you do great and marvelous works!
Enter into His Kingdom and partake in the fruit of His
Majesty, the joy of your royal inheritance!
Amen!

ACKNOWLEDGEMENTS

Special thanks to…

My husband, Jonathan Middleton, for your creative graphic design and professional help in putting this book together.

My parents, Greg and Jane Moore, for your endorsement, editorial help and design consultation.

Our children, Noah, Tyler, Cailyn and Emma, for their testimonies and modeling displayed throughout this book.

Friend and Author, Marian Nygard, for her foreword and review.

Friends, family and pastors who encouraged and celebrated us in the creation of our first book.

ENDORSEMENT

How do you 'change the culture of your nation' in ten years?
By changing a generation of young children who are equipped
and confident enough in Daddy God's character to step out
and see the dead raised, with family and friends healed and
encouraged as a 'normal' way of life. This explosive new book
will set the course of your children's faith and future as they
realize their God given potential through Jesus Christ.

Amazement! That is the reaction of countless parents who
have experienced the reality of God's power released through
their children once Stephanie has taught them how easy it is
for them to heal and prophesy. There is no junior Holy Spirit!
With insight and passion, author, teacher, wife, mother,
daughter and revivalist, Stephanie Middleton, will guide you
into the steps of setting your children on fire for the things of
God that they will carry for a lifetime.

*"Train up a child in the way he should go. Even when he is old he will
not depart from it." Proverbs 22:6*

Greg and Jane Moore
Believing Jesus Ministries

CONTENTS

FOREWORD

I first met Stephanie Middleton a few years back through her parents, Greg and Jane Moore from Believing Jesus Ministries.

Our son, Adrian, had been miraculously healed a year earlier and Stephanie and I were sharing stories of God's fierce love and tender touch. In the course of the evening, I sensed Holy Spirit stirring within me, creating a new longing to go even deeper with God.

When I heard Stephanie telling her story of praying a little child back to life after drowning, my heart cried out for the Kingdom of God to be revealed through my life, for heaven to come to earth through my prayers, and for life to be released through my hands. The testimony of Jesus will do that to you. You never remain the same.

Stephanie's stories of lifeless bodies returning to life, of creative miracles and a lifestyle of healings, encourage me to live in my true identity as a daughter of the living King, created to co-labor with Christ. Coming alongside people of faith will strengthen your own.

Having spent time with Stephanie and witnessed how she champions her children to run with their divine legacy, I am thrilled that she has now made her wisdom and revelation available to other parents. The *ABCs of Healing – Teaching Your Kids to Heal* will encourage you as you raise your children to be bold *first responders* in times of sickness and even death, as they press in to see God's kingdom come and His will be done, on earth as it is in heaven.

We want our children to stand on our shoulders. Nothing makes me happier than seeing my children praying for the sick and handicapped and the Kingdom of God being released through them. I want this to be their normal. I celebrate how they approach the mysteries of God with childlike faith and trusting confidence. They know that if they show up, so will He.

As I followed the pregnancy and birth of the Middleton's youngest daughter, Emma, I wept in grateful awe of the God of miracles. I have proclaimed their testimony over many babies and young lives. God is faithful. He will do it again. It's in His nature.

Take hold of Stephanie's teaching. Carry it in your heart. Write in on your doorposts. Activate your children in a lifestyle of healings. Leave a mark that will stand the test of time. Invest in the generations to come. Glorify the name of Jesus!

Marian Nygard
Author of *I Have a Good Life – The Story of Adrian's Healing*

INTRODUCTION

Like the testimony of the fishes and the loaves, healing happens when we give what we've got and marvelously watch as He brings the increase beyond measure as the name of Jesus is proclaimed upon our lips.

As a former elementary educator, children's ministry leader and now, a parent, I have championed many children into an effortlessly snowballing lifestyle of praying for the sick and seeing the sick healed. Parents of children I have taught, have expressed their amazement and gratitude for their children's spiritual hunger, faith filled beliefs and actions even years later, as they have entered into their teenage years. The ease in which these children have learned how to heal, expect miracles and chosen to couple themselves with Jesus as their Lord and Savior, fearlessly displaying His Kingdom as they go, have often contacted me for the "how tos." Thus, the birth of this book began to take shape and was inspired through much encouragement, prophetic words and dreams through trusted ministers of the faith.

The title of this book is quite fitting, since healing is just as simplistic as the title suggests. Even if you have never prayed for healing yourself, this book will champion you into an easy lifestyle of healing miracles as you learn right alongside your children. In my opinion, practicing with the little ones who Jesus calls into His Kingdom, is the most exciting and rewarding place to start! Learn from the masters of childlike faith as you faithfully steward Kingdom principles that encourage healing in your life and in the lives of your children.

You will learn how to foundationally build upon your children's royal identity as sons and daughters of the King of Kings, teaching them how to pray with A – Authority as Jesus modeled and instructed. You will learn how to cultivate B –Belief in your children as you foster their confidence in the nature and faithfulness of their heavenly Daddy through treasuring and telling the testimonies. You will learn how to position your children to C – Celebrate what God is doing and celebrate one another as you step out to pray for healing together. Living our lives in His companionship and royal authorship, learning to trust in and celebrate His faithfulness, is when we begin to become true victors; walking towards the Hope upon which we were called in our God given destinies.

You were born again for such a time as this! People were meant to see Jesus powerfully displayed through your very vessel! Upon your very breath, His lovely Name, Jesus, releases His Holy Spirit into any given situation in a powerful display of awe and wonder. People will see His glory displayed through all of His children, causing them to know that surely, there must be a God! *"For even out of the mouth of infants and nursing babes, God establishes His strength." Psalm 8:1-2*

Be blessed as you enter into the fruits of your royal inheritance and put healing into practice with your children. *"God promises that you will come short in no gift as the testimony of Jesus is confirmed in you!" 1 Corinthians 1:6-8*

Much love and blessing,

Stephanie Middleton

Chapter 1

Resurrection Life

"But if the Spirit of Him who raised Jesus from the dead dwells in you,
He who raised Christ from the dead will also give life
to your mortal bodies through His Spirit who dwells in you."

Romans 8:11

Heading out of the hotel's front doors, a panicked shriek calls out from behind us, "Oh my gosh! Someone call 9-1-1! The baby drowned!"

We froze, our hearts pounded with the anecdote. *He needs the life of Jesus.* Without hesitation, we turn and run towards the pool doors. Bursting through them, we see a large crowd of people huddled together on the far side of the room. Recognizing an opening in the large mass, we make our way over and 'slide into first' on the wet floor.

There he was, a two or three-year-old little boy, lifeless. He was ghostly white: unmoving. His body appeared as if he was made of rubber. He was dead. A man had tried to administer CPR before our arrival, but it hadn't worked. The little boy was already gone. The scene was surreal.

All around us hung traumatic grief. Some people were crying. Others stood on the outskirts of the small crowd, their mouths gaping in shock. A little girl, her face angry, punched a beach ball into the pool. Against the wall, the mother of the little boy was violently trying to break free from the arms that held her back, screaming out in helpless agony.

All that we could focus on in that moment, was the little boy and the anecdote that we knew we carried. It was the only thing that would bring him back to life. We zeroed in. *He needs the life of Jesus in him* rang in our hearts.

We put our hands on him and boldly prayed "In the name of Jesus, we rebuke the spirit of death and release the resurrection life of Jesus into him." We repeated it two or three times, each time with more confidence in our hearts. Our eyes glued on the lifeless boy in front of us, looking for life to arise.

We put our hands on him and boldly prayed "In the name of Jesus, we rebuke the spirit of death and release the resurrection life of Jesus into him."

All of a sudden, his belly rose up and began to ripple! It made its way up to his chest and lungs. Color came back into his face. His mouth opened and a deep breath drew from his body that was once dead. His eyes opened and he started to look around the room wide eyed and stunned.

"Sit him up! Sit him up!" We yelled. Hands from all around him reached in and helped him to sit up. He slowly looked around as he took in the large number of faces staring at him. Then, he started to cry. His mother, now released, rushed over and scooped her son up into her arms. The people around us, moved in closer, sandwiching Jon and I, into a large group hug.

"EMT. What happened?" we heard a voice say. We turned to see two paramedics walk in, followed by more.

Slightly embarrassed, my husband and I quickly glanced at each other and said "Let's go." So, we left.

The testimony spread like wildfire! As soon as we got to the Jesus Culture conference in Cleveland, Ohio, we were asked to share the Good News of Jesus still at work bringing the dead to life. I got up to share the Good News with the mass of people in attendance. My jeans were still dripping wet from sliding onto the pool floor moments ago, my spirit exhilarated and my nerves dancing at God's miraculous work! Before I could even finish sharing the full testimony, people sprang to their feet, bursting with praise and applause to Jesus! Faith erupted in the auditorium even more as we gave all glory and honor to King Jesus.

Meanwhile, back at the hotel, our parents checked on the status of the little boy. One of the aunts was still poolside staring off into space, totally stunned and shaking her head back and forth. She was dumbfounded at what she had just witnessed in the name of Jesus. She relayed that the EMT reported that the little boy was completely fine as if nothing had ever happened. For insurance reasons, they ran him down to the hospital to get him checked out. Praise Jesus!

The next morning, we had to leave early to get home and pick up our puppy from a friend's house. On our way home, we kept thinking about what happened. It was still really surreal. We hoped that the family knew that it was because of Jesus, that their little boy came back to life. Just then, we got a phone call from my mom.

"Guess what?" She whispered excitedly.

"What?" we wandered.

"I'm sitting next to the grandmother of the little boy that drowned!" mom exclaimed.

"Mom! Don't say anything!"

"No, I won't. Your dad told me not to say anything either. I am out in the hallway. I just wanted to tell you a one sided phone conversation that I could hear from the grandmother of the little boy that drowned." We listened eagerly.

"No, he was dead... He was white... I don't know but I wouldn't trust my boy into the hands of some stranger (probably in reference to the man who attempted to revive him through CPR)...Well, who do you think it was? (God)... Well, alright then... I don't know... Some little white girl flew in from nowhere!"

Hallelujah! They knew it was the Lord and he was alive! Praise Jesus! Our hearts sang! This African American family and friends, approximately thirty people in total, had witnessed the raising of the dead in the name of Jesus!

When we returned home, we didn't tell any of our friends. We didn't want them to know what happened because we thought it would draw unnecessary attention to ourselves. Yet, we quickly repented and realized that the testimony needed to be told! It was not of our own account; it was the account of Jesus still alive and active, testifying that He wants to do it again through the hands of His children who believe in Him and are willing to give it a try.

FIRST GRADER RAISES THE DEAD

I was twenty-six-years-old and a first grade teacher at a diverse, private Christian school. I had already been sharing real life testimonies with my students on healing, the prophetic, God's provision, signs and wonders, angelic encounters, etc. in accordance with Bible stories and activating them in healing, prophetic and the expectation for God to do miracles in their lives and through their very hands.

Children were healing family members, relatives, friends, classmates and even strangers that they encountered in the marketplace with their families. They were prophesying accurately into the lives of their peers and seeing glimpses of Heaven and angels. Children were growing hungry for every testimony that we read in the Bible or shared in class to reproduce in their lives. So, I shared this testimony with my students after sharing Bible stories of Jesus and the disciples raising the dead. They were awestruck.

My students were ecstatic and begged me to tell it to teachers and students that we passed in the hallways, at lunch and at recess time. I had told it to my principal earlier that morning and she had me share it with my peers in a teachers' meeting. I was unsure as to what they would think but it didn't matter. Jesus mattered. His story was worth telling.

After giving account in my classroom about what happened, one little boy who was usually shy and quiet, convinced in disbelief, stated "that's not possible."

"Of course it is!" I said. "Look at what the Bible says!" I shared *Romans 8:11: "But if the Spirit of Him who raised Jesus from the dead dwells in you, He who raised Christ Jesus from the dead will also give life to your mortal bodies through His Spirit who dwells in you."* Tommy didn't say anything in response and we continued about our day.

The next day, he came up to me and said "Mrs. Middleton, I asked my parents and they said that it couldn't happen."

"Okay Tommy, I understand that your parents said it couldn't happen, but, I am just telling you what the Bible says and what happened with me. That it does happen."

A couple weeks later after Spring Break, Tommy, who didn't quite believe that raising the dead was possible, would randomly come up to me and say "Mrs. Middleton, what you said would happen, happened."

"What Tommy? What do you mean?" I tried to get him to elaborate further but I got nothing from him.

One of those times, a little girl named Anna, overheard our conversation and asked "Mrs. Middleton, do you want me to ask Tommy what he's talking about?"

"Yes, Anna, that would be great!" I replied, resuming our lesson. After a few minutes passed, Anna abruptly interrupted our lesson.

"Mrs. Middleton! Mrs. Middleton!"

"What Anna?"

"Tommy raised the dead!"

Tommy went to Ft. Lauderdale, Florida for spring break. His dad and brother were swimming in the pool. The brothers kept commenting about this boy who must be amazing because he was holding his breath for a long time underwater. At first, Tommy's dad didn't think anything of it. Then, after a while, he realized that this couldn't be a good sign.

He dove under the water, secured the boy and powered towards the surface. He pulled him from the pool and propped him up in a nearby chair. There he slumped; an eleven year old boy, his face blue and unresponsive. Tommy's dad started to administer CPR. People were in pandemonium and calling 911.

Tommy stood back watching his father at work to no avail. All of a sudden, he remembered the testimony of the boy who came back to life after drowning in a hotel pool. Tommy knew what to do: he prayed. Tommy said that right after he prayed, the boy came to life.

The boy coughed up water and breathed. The squad that was called, arrived shortly after to assess the situation. The story made one of the papers and Tommy brought it in the following day to share with the class.

PRINCIPAL STEPS OUT ON THE TESTIMONY

My principal, Genie, had heard the testimony and shortly after, attended a healing conference to hear two men of faith ministering at a church in Ohio. The powerful men of God shared about the authority that we have received as sons and daughters of our heavenly Dad. That it's His will to heal and bring the dead to life through His beloved sons and daughters. The message and my testimony embedded in her heart.

Later that week, she was at a store, getting ready to check out. "Someone help me!" a lady in front of her screamed. Genie looked at the panic stricken mother who was screaming and saw a convulsing, blue baby in her arms.

She grabbed the baby out of the mother's arms and started speaking in tongues over the little one. Instantly, she heard in her heart what one man had asked at the conference, *"Do you want to raise the dead?" Yes!* Her heart replied.

Genie began to rebuke death and release life. Instantaneously, the baby stopped convulsing. Her color returned to normal and she breathed normally. The power of Jesus was released. The baby, whose signs of life were failing fast, was immediately restored in perfect Peace. Hallelujah! The mother, the cashier and the other onlookers were made privy at the power of Jesus' name.

OUR HEAVENLY BIRTHRIGHT

As believers, we have been given dominion over the earth, power and authority to heal the sick, raise the dead, cleanse the lepers and cast out devils.[1] We are commissioned for signs and wonders to be released in the nations, that all might come to know Him and receive Him as their Lord and Savior.[2] We have access to the fullness of God's Kingdom and we are privileged to know and steward the mysteries of God.[3]

We are blessed to be one with Him.[4] Wherever we go, He goes and His Spirit is always fully alive inside of us.[5] We are carriers of His Presence, seated in heavenly places beside the King of Kings.[6] Jesus is always interceding for us.[7] We have an entourage of angels guarding all of our ways and their job is to help us administer the Kingdom.[8]

We are sons and daughters, instruments of righteousness, with a promised living crown of glory to wear upon our heads.[9] All of our needs are fully provided for and there is always more than enough in the storehouses of Heaven.[10] God's grace and favor is upon our lives and we reign in fullness of joy, peace and righteousness.[11] We are the apple of our Daddy's eyes and He does more than all we can ask or imagine.[12] We are Daddy's kids and it is His good pleasure to give us the Kingdom.[13]

> *"We are Daddy's kids and it is His good pleasure to give us the Kingdom.*

Our Heavenly Daddy is in the business of bringing the dead to life.[14] He gave us His Son, Jesus, to fulfill the law and conquer death on our behalf so that we may live free from condemnation.[15] He called us by His virtue and glory to walk in victory from faith to faith.[16] On top of that, He declared that *we will do even greater works than Jesus did!* [17] We've got His mighty Spirit inside of us, so, let's release Him and see the mighty deeds He performs. *"For the earnest expectation of the creation eagerly waits for the revealing of the sons of God." Romans 8:19*

ACTIVATIONS

At the end of each chapter, there will be three activation sections entitled:

- Ponder the Possibilities
- Proclaim
- Be Fruitful and Multiply

These are designed to open up childlike wonder with Daddy God and align hearts and minds with Heaven; providing some practical ways that you can step out with your children to practice healing with confident expectation. Be excited! What God starts, He always finishes. He is both Alpha and Omega; Beginning and End.

PONDER THE POSSIBILITIES

You have just read accounts of the dead being raised through a twenty something, a seven-year-old and a fifty something. God says that all of His people can raise the dead because we have been given the ministry of life through His Spirit! That means you and the very children whom the Lord has given you!

Spend some time in thanksgiving with the Lord and imagine the adventurous possibilities with Him. Write down what you are seeing, hearing, feeling, etc.

What statements stand out to you in this first chapter of 'Resurrection Life?'

Take note on how each person released resurrection life. Ask God for opportunities to release His life giving power through you and your children!

PROCLAIM

Read through 'Our Heavenly Birthright' section substituting 'I' for the word 'we.' Declare these truths over yourself out loud.

Now, repeat these proclamations by inserting your child's name into these sentences.

What is being awakened to life inside of you?

BE FRUITFUL AND MULTIPLY

Tell your children an account of Jesus raising the dead with great excitement and anticipation. Tell them that *what Jesus did, He'll do again. And if Jesus did it, you will too.* Share the testimonies of the teacher, the little boy and the principal with them. As you share these testimonies, re-enact them out as if you are the ones praying for resurrection life.

Ask your children, *"If Jesus raised the dead and said you can do it, can you?"*

Encourage your children that God has big plans for them and that God is going to move powerfully through them to display Heaven on earth and call the dead to life. Now, let's get started.

Chapter 2

Let the Children Come

"But Jesus said, 'Let the little children come to Me, and do not forbid them; for of such is the Kingdom of Heaven.'"

Matthew 19:14

C hildren are purposed to be empowered heirs of the Kingdom of Heaven, reigning in all of His righteousness, peace and joy.[18] Children so easily embody innocence, wonder, creativity, hope, justice, love, joy, trust, generosity, adventures and the list continues. These characteristics are a prime launching pad for the Lord to display His love and glory all over the earth. Heaven invading earth is meant to be released through every person that receives Jesus as Lord and Savior, be it young or old.[19] We believe that the greatest revival of all time is about to happen with children joining the ranks and leading the way with Father's heart and blessing.

The Kingdom of heaven is superior to that of the natural mind. Yet, it is very simple to access.[20] In fact, in Matthew 18:3 Jesus says that it is childlikeness that invites the reign of Heaven to earth. He says "Assuredly, I say to you, unless you are converted and become as little children, you will by no means enter the kingdom of heaven."

Pondering this verse unravels one's mind back to the basics. It's interesting because Jesus makes this simple statement right after the disciples asked Him which one of them were the greatest. They were all great, but surely one of them had to be greater. Jesus is quick to address them as they are missing the profound Good News of the Gospel. Upon their asking, Jesus pulls a child in from the outskirts of their wanderings and places him right in the middle of their group. Jesus says *look, if you want the full reign of the heavens on earth, than you have got to convert and become childlike.* What did Jesus even mean by this?

The word converted in this text is the Greek word *strephó* meaning to turn about.[21] He is pointing out that their mindset is limiting them from entering into the fullness of the Kingdom. It's almost as if Jesus is saying *you think what you've tasted so far is good, but I have got news for you there is more. If you want the fullness of Heaven demonstrated upon the earth, repent. Enter in like a child.*[22]

> *If you want the fullness of Heaven demonstrated upon the earth, repent. Enter in like a child.*

The disciples were probably caught completely off guard as so much of Jesus' profound, simple statements often times do. These close friends were starting to look at greatness in the Kingdom from a worldly viewpoint; looking at success and greatness in the Kingdom through a tiered lens based on their ever growing knowledge and track record with Him in an outward comparison to their peers around them. Their minds were deductively making sense of His miraculous greatness displayed through them; trying to establish the reason for the how or why. If they chosen to level off in rank in their own justified understanding before men, then their receiving would have leveled off as well. It is God who justifies us by the faith seed found within. His glory boldly displayed upon our surrendered lives. "*...If man should glory, let him glory in the Lord.*" *2 Corinthians 10:12-17*

Through God's mercy and loving kindness, His free gift has raised us up together that we may abound in all things with Him. It's not of our own works that we should boast but in the immeasurable works of the Lord continuing to manifest through our measurable bodies.[23] While the Word of the Lord beholds boundless mystery, there are some powerful things we can make note about what it looks like to be childlike.

KINGDOM IN CHILDREN

First, children in the eyes of the world are weak. Children are dependent upon the One that supplies. They don't view their weaknesses as limitations. Every time children recognize that they need strength and wisdom outside of their own abilities, they ask. Instead of staring in the face of their own weaknesses and insufficiencies, they look at the face of His strength and all sufficiency.[24]

Believing oneself to have fully arrived in the Kingdom actually prevents it from manifesting in greater measure. If one is great, there is no need for supply, no need for growth and no need for submission. He is the Great I am, His greatness made to stand upon our weakness as a platform for the world to see that Jesus Christ is Lord.[25]

Adults tend to initially see their own weaknesses as limitations. This inward focus disempowers the Kingdom being displayed through us. It causes us to timidly carry the Pearl of Great Price like a clam. When placed in new environments or situations, we clam up from fear. Our focus is shifted inwards onto ourselves for the answer instead of our eyes drawn upwards to Him for the Answer.[26] *"What's sown in weakness, is raised in power." 1 Corinthians 15:43*

Second, a child growing up in a healthy environment of true love is never basing his or her identity in comparison with those around them. Their track record does not determine who they are. A child innately carries a confidence in who they are for they are fearfully and wonderfully made in His image. There is not even a temptation to believe lies that would persuade them to think otherwise. When children see great things happening through others, they are ecstatic! It opens their minds to what's possible and invites them in to experience that same greatness: an adventure to be had! Children's identities rest in the One who loves them, their destinies cemented in His promises and their hopes securely encouraged in His faithful nature. Surrounded by others who are like minded, they edify each other through encouragement. Their teammates fuel their perseverance to finish the race marked out for them. It's not a me or them mentality, it's an us in Him mentality.

Walking into the middle of a young child's sporting event, it's not immediately recognizable as to who is winning or who is the greatest. Comparison hasn't shown its face, advanced moves or the score of the game doesn't determine one's greatness. Children are thrilled and invincible working together to conquer the task at hand. There is no fear of the outcome because they are freely confident in their present, unmeasured ability to perform what's in front of them. A familiar strength resides within them, conditioned by their coach as they are cheered on by those around them. Victory is victory both corporately and individually; a win for the team!

Playing sports not only requires athletic skill, but the heart and mind to persevere. Even if it's a child's teammate who regularly hits the home runs while they always strike out, they are not easily shaken. A child's identity isn't influenced by their ability to perform. Their eyes remain fixed on the love of the game. It's the love of the game that fuels their drive to keep going and it's the Love of Jesus, that fuels our drive to keep going forward in Him.[27]

Ranking ourselves in understanding or experience caps off that which is free flowing from the throne of God. Our greatness is imprisoned when we compare ourselves with those around us, our destinies hindered and disillusioned as we have unknowingly put God in a box. We falsely believe Him to be "all known" when His Word clearly points out *who can understand the ways of God? (paraphrase Romans 11:33)*

Romans 11:33 says "Oh, the depth of the riches both of the wisdom and knowledge of God! How unsearchable are His judgments and His ways past finding out!" He is the only One Who is all knowing.[28] Repentance is the only tool that will unlock the chains that prevent us from moving freely in Him and discovering more of His marvelous mystery.[29]

Third, a child accepts truth from trusted people unreservedly. Children trust people who hold true to their word and do not veer from it no matter the circumstance. As a person's actions continuously line up with their words, their heart is revealed in the process. Trust is developed through intimacy as faithfulness continues to prove itself with each new experience.

GO ON HIS FAITHFULNESS

We release the Kingdom with ease when we focus on His Truth telling and His faithfulness.[30] He is Who He says He is and He will do what He says He will do. Our feet can go confidently in that and we see Him when we move, because our eyes are focused on Him. He proves Himself faithful, His nature and word unchanged by the circumstance; Heaven released on every occasion.

It is like the testimony recorded in Mark 14, when Jesus walks towards His disciples on the sea. When His friends see Him, they are all afraid that He is a ghost. This figure looks like Jesus but it's a totally new event and it terrifies them. Peter sees the same occurrence and even though He is unsure of it, He asks the Lord if it's Him. He has learned to know the Lord as he has walked with Him. So, Peter says *'Lord, I will know it's You, if You tell me to come.'* Jesus tells Him to *come*. Peter knows it's Jesus, so, his feet can follow.

We release the Kingdom with ease when we focus on His Truth telling and faithfulness.

The story proceeds to tell us how the surrounding atmosphere – the waves, the wind start to draw his eyes off of the Steadfast One. He looks at the chaos around Him and allows fear to creep in. Thus, he start to sink. Jesus reaches out His hand and says "Oh you of little faith, why did you doubt?" It sounds a little harsh but Jesus is simply saying *Oh you of little confidence in me, why did you not believe that I would do it?* Our faith is based in His faithfulness, not on our own. And, the instability around us is the very thing that attracts the Peace of Heaven.

Faith is produced by our belief in Him. My parents of Believing Jesus ministries say that "faith is our confidence in Him." Their powerful statement is expounded upon when they share the definition of faith in *Webster's* Dictionary as having confidence in a person's character. When presented with new opportunities, we fix our eyes on His nature and His faithfulness. This is how one attains faith, the currency to draw from Heaven's bank account of limitless supply - password Jesus!

Hebrews 11:1 says "Faith is the substance of things hoped for, the evidence of things not seen." When we fix our eyes on Jesus – who He is, what He has done and remain expectant of what He promises He'll do, the substance of Hope is here and faith is accredited on our behalf. Looking to Him, we can step out in complete confidence, knowing that it's Him at work in us. If our eyes remain focused on what He's doing, we will see Him do something. The next time we behold a new opportunity, we can look at His faithfulness in our history and step out once again. This is how we move from faith to faith, confidence to confidence. If we, as children can see His perfect history and step out on that, then we'll see His story take shape before our eyes and through our hands into eternity. Forever and ever, Amen.

> *If our eyes remain focused on what He's doing, we will see Him do something.*

ACCEPT HIS TRUTHS

Children easily accept truths. What a child accepts as truth instantly changes the way they see things. The way they see things is the influencer for how they will act. Destiny, determined by the seeds embedded within.

The parables in the Bible are destiny seeds. Mysterious Kingdom truths and principles continually revealed through such simple, yet profound stories. They reveal His heart and the nature on which His fruitful Kingdom operates and expands. This is how we are renewing our minds, by allowing these truths to gently embed in our hearts and continually remaining open to what He's revealing on an ever growing basis. This is what will help us to grow up in the fullness of Christ.

The Gospel of the Living God is mind blowing. We tremble at His glory. Yet, we are completed vessels purposed to carry and express this incredible greatness.[31] It's beyond comprehension, ready within ourselves and so easy to release. He tells us simply, *"receive it as children."*

The parables are paradigm shifters. They are awakening people to how life operates under the King's domain, Grace. Jesus teaches about Grace and He says that our way into it, is simply receiving what He says as Truth.[32] Truth changes the way we see things and acts as the rudder for how we go.[33] Accept it as children.

GIVE WHAT YOU'VE GOT

The testimony of the fishes and loaves is a powerful example that the Kingdom begins with childlikeness. There were masses of people gathered to hear, see and be touched by Jesus. Only the number of men present are recorded: five thousand. It is getting late and people are getting hungry. The disciples come to Jesus and ask Him what they should do. The logical answer would be to send them home. Yet, Jesus says something even more radical "You feed them." They look at themselves for they have nothing, no money and no food. The price tag on such a task is beyond a year's wage.

The solution, still unidentified at the time, remains with a child. The child upon hearing the need doesn't think twice. Upon hearing the need, he simply recognizes that he has something that he can give and delivers it to Jesus. Then, Jesus brings the increase beyond measure. He graciously allows the miracle to take place within the hands of his learners as they distribute it to the hungry people, partakers of the Bread of Life. This is a powerful testimony that as the bread is broken, it's more than enough to feed everyone with twelve heaping baskets left over!

Jesus' body was broken on the cross for us. Not only does He fill those who come to fellowship with Him, but there is still more than enough to keep partaking in with Him.[34] He came for the masses and his supply isn't found on the earth but released from His unending heavenly supply. His Kingdom of increase beyond measure is accessed, when we recognize that we have got something to give and partner with Him to bring what's needed to fruition.

PART OF THE SOLUTION

Children are ready for the Kingdom! [35] His Word declares the full reign of the Heavens accessed through childlikeness and His Kingdom designed to receive them. If we want the full reign of Heaven on earth, then even our children need to be aware of who they are and what they have to give. We must train our children in the atmosphere and knowledge of Grace, so when they see a problem, they recognize that they carry the solution! When they step out to pray and release what they've got, Jesus brings the increase beyond measure. [36] He loves to let His beloved sons and daughters who are always learning, be a part of His miracles. [37] We have been commissioned to be part of the solution that reveals the Answer to the world, Jesus Christ.

> *We must train our children in the atmosphere and knowledge of Grace, so when they see a problem, they recognize that they carry the solution!*

One can liken it to an algebra problem. Jesus Christ is the Answer for everything. We can solve for x, the Kingdom revealed, when we realize that we are part of the solution. We are the given number. We being derived from Him, work out our salvation from the Answer to the problem, revealing Heaven's solution. That which is unseen is made clearly seen. Jesus is alive and His Heaven on earth is here now, through our partnership with His Holy Spirit.

Jesus is so kind. He is the Answer for everything. He'll release His Kingdom on us even if we are unaware of who we are -

part of the solution that all of creation has been groaning for.[38] He'll nudge us with His Presence, awakening us to who we are.

We can't be an unknown variable! No basic mathematician can fully know the Answer, if they are looking at two unknowns. It doesn't make sense to the natural mind. The world can't fully know Jesus, if we don't allow ourselves to be a part of the equation. Heaven is meant to be revealed through us, working it out with the Answer in mind.[39]

AN INVITATION

In life we may be stirred by newness, yet we are settled by Grace. We carry the familiar knowing, Holy Spirit, that God is with us. *"If He is for us, who can be against us?" Romans 8:31* Undone by His generous heart that He who loves us would give His Spirit without measure to rest in imperfect vessels who are continually being perfected by the story of His death and resurrection.[40] His gentle whispers breathing life on our hearts, *I am in you. I am He who overcame the world. I am your Peace and I will lead you onward in Christ Jesus. Together, we can do anything for I am the God of incalculable possibilities.* Be childlike in your love, in your identity, in your trust, in your hope and most importantly, in your God.

We've all been invited to partake in this glorious mystery. At times, it may seem uncertain but our Constant, is ever present. Uncertainty extends its hand into greater intimacy should we choose to accept; a knowing of the Bridegroom, the Victorious One. His Kingdom come is the marriage bed of delighted Love and Life. We are purposed in Him and for Him; purposed for His Kingdom to be released through us. Not having it all figured out or being able to do something on our own accord is wonderful because it means we need Him to be a part of our lives. Uncertain? Champion the children around you to lead them into more of His Kingdom. Learn and grow together. Let us enter in one accord. *"For the promise is for you and your children and for all who are far off, as many as the Lord will call to Himself." Acts 2:39* Hallelujah!

PONDERING THE POSSIBILITIES

What does it look like to be childlike?

Do you know that you are already a child? What ways do you embrace childlikeness in His Kingdom? What ways do you have difficulty being childlike in His Kingdom? How will you reposition yourself to continually be childlike in His Kingdom?

Spend time with God and ask Him to show you how your children are powerful.

In what ways does their childlikeness present opportunities for the Kingdom to be displayed? How is He moving powerfully in them right now?

Ask Holy Spirit to show you some ways to position them to experience the fullness of His Kingdom, the fruit of His Majesty.

PROCLAIM

God is Who He says He is and He'll do what He says He'll do.

God is faithful every time and He moves faithfully through me.

I am a son/daughter of the Most High God and He delights in me all of the time.

God is with me and is proud to be known through me.

He is my greatest encourager.

I've got something to give. He brings the increase.

I am purposed to be a part of the equation, bringing Heaven to earth. His Kingdom is made manifest as I work out my salvation with Him in mind.

He shows up every time.

BE FRUITFUL AND MULTIPLY

Create a value to honor and protect the childlike awe, wonder and expectation of God. Dream with God. Imagine you and your children healing various people who are crippled, lame, sick, dead, etc. Where it seems like an impossibility, practice repentance and ask God to give you words or pictures for what's possible with Him. What did you see or hear?

Ask God to invite you into opportunities to experience the power and authority that you've been given.

Incorporate encouraging your children through verbal praise of their courage and childlikeness in different situations. Call out the gold you see in them and the ways that you see the fruits of His Spirit manifesting in their lives. Continue to do that to the people that you daily encounter too.

Chapter 3

A is for Authority

"…All authority has been given to Me in Heaven and on earth. Go therefore and make disciples of all the nations, baptizing them in the name of the Father and of the Son and of the Holy Spirit, teaching them to observe all things that I have commanded you; and lo, I am with you always, even to the end of the age." Amen.

Matthew 28:18-20

I n the New Testament, the Bible says numerous times that people were amazed and marveled at the authority Jesus carried. They constantly referenced that His authority was similar to that found in the testimonies of Moses, yet greater.

In the land of Egypt, Pharaoh was given all authority. Moses as a royal member of Pharaoh's household was groomed all throughout his youth in knowing his princely authority. He learned that what he said and carried was done without question. When he heard the Lord's voice, he received strategy from Heaven to lead a nation out of bondage to the promise land. Moses stepped out in full confidence, knowing that the Lord was going to perform what He said He would.

Moses is a prophetic picture of what has now been made available to every believer, regardless of age or gender through the death and resurrection of Jesus Christ. God also says that we will do greater works than Jesus did. It is time for all of God's children to be trained up in their authority to lead powerfully and successfully with their heavenly Daddy, God Almighty.

GREATER WORKS THAN JESUS

In the Great commission, Jesus says that all authority in heaven and earth has been given to Him and He released it on His disciples, royal members of the household of God.[41] Disciples, *mathētēs*, literally means His learners.[42] As believers, we are constantly learning and growing in the Kingdom and we can groom our children all throughout their youth in knowing their royal authority just like Moses.[43]

Father has graciously bestowed upon us His authority, with His seal of approval, Holy Spirit to accomplish even greater things than Jesus did.[44] We may not always get it right, but all things are constantly being made right in His name. Expect great things to happen as you teach your children to step out in the powerful authority bestowed upon them.

PRACTICE IT

When teaching children to pray, from tots to teens, we have found it very effective in our ministry by teaching children how to pray from authority. Just like the testimony of the fishes and the loaves, authority recognizes that we've got something to give and responds accordingly. Authority is learned from hearing, seeing, modeling and hands on practicing. It's how the disciples learned from Jesus and it's a successful, research based model for how children effectively learn and become successful lifelong learners. *Philippians 4:9 says "The things you have learned and received and heard and seen in me, practice these things, and the God of peace will be with you."*

When modeling and practicing healing with children, it is important to create a safe and encouraging learning environment, where every person is valued.[45] Every opportunity to pray is exciting, positive and encouraging. Be a cheerleader!

COMMAND IT IN JESUS' NAME

I personally started to step out in healing when I became aware that it was available and believed that I was purposed to do it. I began to see success in healing when my mom would pull me into her opportunities to pray for people. She had me put my hands on people and repeat after her, commanding prayers in Jesus' name, demonstrating Kingdom authority. It was through her modeling it and practicing it with me that I began to know that He would move through me to heal others.

My mom pioneered our family into moving in signs and wonders with Him. She positioned herself as a child. She fully believed the Lord and believed that she was able to perform what He commissioned her to do in His Word. The lack of healing she was seeing or experiencing wasn't the determining factor for whether or not she could heal, Jesus was. The lack of healing fueled her hunger, compelling her to put everything she learned into practice. As a result, she began to see healing in increasing measure! Now, she sees whole healings regularly.

My mom stewards Heaven well. What she receives, she gives away all for the love of her Father and Friend. Her safeguarded childlike wonder, trust and hope continues to launch her into phenomenal healing testimonies that occur on a regular basis. It was her perseverance to see healing. It was her desire to see her family move in healing. It was her encouraging leadership that pulled us into opportunities to practice it that made it come to life. My dad was quick to follow suit, my brother and I close behind.

Together, my mom and dad began to pursue this normal lifestyle of His Kingdom made manifest not only for themselves, but for others too. As they found their ease with Him, they shared and taught others. Their favor continuously increases with God and man as they give away what they've been given from Father. They are true cheerleaders and coaches of the faith as they truly desire to see everyone reach their fullness in Christ and share Him with the nations through His miraculous works.

It was in one of their schools, that they shared one of Jesus' teachings found in John 14:10-14, that gave life and confidence to what I had been practicing in Him. It reads *"Do you not believe that I am in the Father, and the Father in Me? The words that I speak to you I do not speak on my own authority; but the Father who dwells in Me does the works. Believe Me that I am in the Father and the Father in Me, or else believe Me for the sake of the works themselves. Most assuredly, I say to you, he who believes in Me, the works that I do he will do also; and greater works than these he will do because I go to My Father. And whatever you ask in My name, that I will do, that the Father may be glorified in the Son. If you ask anything in My name, I will do it.' "*

They shared that when this passage says *whatever you ask*, it translates as the word require or command. So whatever you command in His name, He will do.[46] Commanding prayers are unnatural if we don't know that we possess the royal right to give them.

Jesus clearly mandated that authority has been given to us through Him and we must exercise it. Jesus modeled it so we could practice it. Jesus ordained it so we could decree it. As a result, we get to see great works displayed in His name. This is how I have come to walk in healing in my own life and have championed the children whom the Lord has given me to pray for healing. All of them have experienced healing through their hands.

CREATE A CULTURE THAT VALUES HEALING

Jesus mandated that authority has been given to us through Him and we must exercise it. Jesus modeled it so we could practice it. Jesus ordained it so we could decree it.

When we weren't even fully confident in healing yet, we made it a priority in our family culture to always pray for healing every time our babies got hurt. We would kiss and cuddle them and dress any wounds if needed in the natural but it was always in the initial consoling that we would always pray. We would say something like "Daddy God, pain go. Head heal. In Jesus' name, amen." Usually our babies would still be crying afterwards.

Our first son, Noah, had barely started walking and couldn't even talk yet. He fell down and got hurt. He was bawling uncontrollably and ran up to me. I was discouraged that every time I had prayed, he still cried afterwards. I believed the lie that my previous efforts had no healing effects. So, I inwardly decided that I wasn't going to pray for him this time. He abruptly grabbed my hand, placed it on his head and waited for me to pray. I was shocked! My prayers must have had some effect or he wouldn't want me to pray! So, I prayed for him. Noah immediately stopped crying and ran away. It was at that moment that I knew to keep pressing in. The Lord was at work regardless of what I was seeing or experiencing.[47] Our prayers do not return void. *"So this is my Word that goes out from mouth: It will not return to me empty, but will accomplish what I desire and achieve the purpose for which I sent it." Isaiah 55:11*

A few months later, we were vacationing at Lake Cumberland and had docked our boat at Jamestown marina to wait out a small storm. My mom sat down in a corner of the store, her knee in a lot of pain. She called out "Stephanie, can you come pray for me? My knees are in a lot of pain and it is hard to put pressure on them."

Before I could respond, Noah walking by, outstretched his hand and placed it on her knee. All he could say was "Jesus' name."

My mom, amazed, stood up and exclaimed "the pain left!" With our young children, we continue to encourage praying for healing. This practice has already become a part of their core value system. They don't even think twice about praying for their own injuries or praying for others. It has become their first response and our family has witnessed many healings through their hands as a result.

Our second son, Tyler, was two years old. He was playfully wrestling with his aunt Ruth. Tyler jumped off of the couch to dive onto her tummy. Ruth was in the middle of turning onto her side and Tyler hit his head on her shoulder with a loud thud! Despite his own extreme pain, he immediately reached over to first pray for Ruth and then himself. Aunt Ruth was so touched.

We have modeled healing and practiced healing as a part of our every day when the opportunity presents itself. Now, our children have taken ownership in the role of releasing healing through Jesus. It has become a natural response in any situation.

Whether teaching children at school, church or home, we make it a high priority to practice praying for healing and for God to miraculously provide throughout the course of our day, as a need arises. An excellent coach looks for opportunities that his team can seize in order to excel in their game. We grab every opportunity we recognize as an invitation to partner with God and see His Kingdom come right now.[48]

When our boys were one and two years old, our family attended a small group of married couples with children ranging from babies to young toddlers. One little tot came to group that week with his leg in a cast. He had just gotten it that very week. Before it was time for everyone to leave to head home, I summoned the tiny tots to gather around the boy with the injured leg, to pray for healing. I had them place their hands on his leg and told them that we were going to pray for his leg to get better. With their hands placed on their friend's leg, we said a quick prayer. Then, we packed up to leave.

The next week at group, that same little boy returned with his family but he didn't have on his cast anymore. I asked what happened and his mom said "He was supposed to have it on for at least another couple of weeks but the doctor said he didn't need it anymore." Wow! God is so good and he loves to heal through our hands regardless of whether we fully understand or not.

We must place a high value on cultivating healing with our children by looking for opportunities to demonstrate God's extravagant goodness to heal through their able hands so they can know Him in a tangible, powerful way. Healing is a natural by-product of our relationship with Jesus and practicing it throughout our daily lives in our family culture and in the marketplace, empowers our children to look to God and pray first as their new normal response and approach to life. Seeing healing and miracles on a regular, increasing basis is not as we pause, but as we go. Empowering a fearless generation, comfortable and confident for the manifest Presence of God to work through their very vessels.[49]

Seeing healing and miracles on a regular, increasing basis is not as we pause, but as we go.

The parable of the talents is an excellent example of how the Kingdom is deposited on earth through His faithful servants. The ones that put the Kingdom to use as they go about their daily lives will see a return on all of their efforts.[50] The Kingdom made manifest through His stewards of Heaven, people's lives and bodies, forever transformed. To Him be the glory forever and ever, amen!

GIVE IT A GO

We love how our parents championed the practice of healing in us and in others. They highlight the Great Commission given by Jesus to all of His disciples by *saying "And as you go, preach, saying 'The Kingdom of Heaven is at hand. Heal the sick, cleanse the lepers, raise the dead, cast out demons. Freely you have received, freely give."* Matthew 10:7-8 They emphasize a paraphrased definition of *go* in *Webster's* Dictionary saying it means: *Give it a try! Make an attempt! Proceed, and pass it along!*

As you go throughout your daily life with your children, take hold of opportunities to pray for healing and pray for miracles. Jesus continuously modeled it to his disciples for three years before they started doing it on their own. It was through repetition that the practice became routine.

Repetition fosters the most intuitive principle of learning and is one of the most notably effective methods for teaching students. Repetition actually transforms things in your brain so when you are presented with the same stimulus, you respond in the practiced manner without a second thought.

Every child will excel in healing with practice. Some children might take ownership of it right away and others a little longer. Yet, everyone is invited to the table and everyone can eat.[51] Persevere. Don't give up! If you value it, model it and practice it with your children, they will get it! You'll both be blessed as you give it a go together.

AUTHORITY IN ROYAL IDENTITY

With children I have taught over the years, I am continually reminding them of who they are and what they have been given. It's almost a daily practice. I usually say "If Daddy God is your Father, you are His son or daughter. And, if He is the King of all Kings, what does that make you? I wait for them to respond with a prince or princess. Then, I continue on stating that if they are sons and daughters of God, princes and princesses, they have fully received everything in His Kingdom. After reminding them of their identity and what they've been given, I remind them of what they can do. We'll talk about the testimonies of Jesus. We talk about what happened in the Bible, what is continuing to happen today and what He will do. Then, I ask them if Jesus said you'll do greater works than He did, will you? *Yes! Yes! Yes!* They always exclaim; their hearts burning with fiery hunger for more of Heaven. Thank You Jesus!

The basis for signs and wonders rests with Man of Truth. It all comes down to do you believe Him and who you are in Him?

The basis for signs and wonders rests with the Man of Truth.[52] It all comes down to do you believe Him and who you are in Him? He is our Confidence, the Author and Perfector of our faith.[53] There will always be new situations to step out in that terrify us like Peter getting out of the boat to walk on water towards Jesus. Yet, every time we step out on His goodness, knowing we have got something to give, His Holy Spirit living in us, we can be sure we are stepping out on a solid foundation. Even if we falter, Jesus will always reach out His hand to lift us up.[54]

BORN TO WALK WITH HIM

We've treasured watching our children grow up as babies. Our daughter, Cailyn, was quick to try and catch up to her big brothers. She started crawling at five months, took steps at seven months and began to walk at ten months old. She knew she was one of us from the beginning. She saw us walk and somehow she instinctively discerned she was destined to walk too. As Cailyn moved about, strength and muscles developed, connections between her brain and body increased. Cailyn went from rolling to crawling, crawling to standing, from standing to walking. During those times when she attempted to walk and fell, she wasn't swayed from believing she was able to do that which she was created to carry out. The thought never even crossed her mind that it wasn't a possibility. Cailyn knew she was one of us, destined and designed to walk effortlessly.

We must see and know that we are made in His image, predestined to walk effortlessly with Him all the days of our lives.[55] All throughout the Old Testament, it references Adam and Eve, Moses, Noah and many others as walking with God as a normal part of their everyday life. We are invited to effortlessly walk with Him in our day in profound mystery and great works.

Children of the Living God, ordained to be vessels of His Presence and releasers of His Kingdom. We are walking testimonies of His life made manifest through Jesus' death and resurrection.[56] His glory is made manifest to those who are about to know Him as Lord and Savior through us. Let's put one foot in front of the other and get walking, because that is how we learn as imitators of Christ, that is how Heaven is released and that is how people will be saved on the earth.

GOD CONFIRMS YOU

This is my prayer and declaration of Truth spoken over you from Father found in *1 Corinthians 1:4-9: "I thank my God always concerning you for the grace of God which was given to you by Christ Jesus, that you were enriched in everything by Him in all utterance and all knowledge, even as the testimony of Christ was confirmed in you, so that you come short in no gift, eagerly waiting for the revelation of our Lord Jesus Christ, who will also confirm you to the end, that you may be blameless in the day of our Lord Jesus Christ. God is faithful, by whom you were called into the fellowship of His Son, Jesus Christ our Lord."*

PONDER THE POSSIBILITIES

What was Moses groomed in throughout his youth? Why do you think it was important?

What was made available to us through Jesus without measure? What does He promise us that we will do with Him?

What does it mean to be a disciple of God? How do you create a safe, encouraging environment that places a high value on being His disciple? Remember, Kingdom success is the act of just giving it a go – not our perceived pass or fail results.

How do you pray with authority? Make it a priority to practice it.

How do you get to experience more of His Kingdom come on the earth?

Write down what you notice from some of the testimonies shared in this chapter about practicing authority. Ask God to show you how you can actively practice authority with your children.

Will you believe what you are seeing or not seeing as truth OR will you let Jesus be the bottom line, the Truth that you will choose to move on every time? Ponder this and make a non-negotiable for the Truth you have the right to move upon. How you will empower this Kingdom reality as you teach your children to pray?

PROCLAIM

I will do greater works than Jesus did.

All authority on heaven and earth has been given to me through Jesus.

Whatever I command in His name to be healed, He will heal.

God acts on my behalf and confirms me to the end.

I am a son/daughter of the King of Kings.

I am a prince/princess and have access to all of Heaven.

God loves it when I give it a go!

God is Truth. God is the Way. God is Life.

I come short in no gift.

I walk with God.

BE FRUITFUL AND MULTIPLY

Take every opportunity to pray for healing. Be expectant. Pray when opportunities arise with your children at home. Pray when opportunities arise with your children as you go. Invite them to pray too.

Don't shame yourself from practicing. If you feel comfortable practicing privately in opportunities that arise at home, start there. As you gain confidence in God's ability to move through you and show up as you move at home, begin to step out as you see opportunities outside of your home. This is how you move from faith to faith, confidence to confidence.

Practice Authoritative Prayers. Some examples are listed on the back of this page.

Starting Questions:

Where does it hurt? If it hurts, on a scale from 1 to 10, 10 being extremely painful, what level of pain are you at right now? Pray. Ask the person to test it out. Thank Daddy God and pray again if needed.

What's not working right? What can't he or she do? Pray for restored mobility and function. Ask the person to test it out. Thank God and pray again if needed.

Example of How to Pray:

"Daddy God, thank You for _____. I release the Kingdom of Heaven into this man's *arm*. I command all pain to go right now. I command all the bones to line up into alignment and that all nerves be unpinched. We speak peace to the muscles, tendons and ligaments and command full mobility and strength to be restored to Heaven's original design in Jesus' name, Amen."

Have the person to test it out and give thanks to God.

Chapter 4

B is for Believe

"And these signs follow those who believe…"

Mark 16:17

The basis for believing is found in the testimonies. Treasuring and telling the testimonies is what builds a firm foundation. A proven track record with Him, launches us into our destinies, knits our hearts to His, teaches us to rely upon His faithfulness and good character.[57]

In the Old Testament, whenever it talks about the Israelites sinning it mentions how it was because they had forgotten the testimony. Every time they were re-directed to His faithfulness of what He had done, it brought them into alignment with His nature and created an expectancy and a place of Him showing up in every situation, no matter the circumstance. The testimonies lead the Israelites out of bondage and into freedom, out of hopelessness into hope, out of the desert and into the Promise Land. How many of us want this in the lives of our children? Wow! Praise Jesus!

My parents believed and experienced God as real and personal throughout their lives. They desired my brother, Stephen and I, to know Him as real and personal in our own lives too. We learned a lot about God throughout our childhood and in our innocence and trust, believed in Him. Yet, our parents wanted even more for us. They wanted us to not only believe His Word, but to know His Word through having our own personal encounters with God. That the Living God would become a tangible and active Presence in our lives.

So, every Sunday morning after we got out of Sunday School class and were waiting beside our parents for them to take us home, they would purposefully strike up conversations that would attune our ears to His testimonies and mysteries. Most of the time, their conversations were with their friend, a well-respected scientist. My mom and dad would say "Carl, tell us again what you told us earlier about God showing up." And, he would graciously share his godly stories with us while we listened intently.

My brother, Stephen and I, learned more from those accounts than we did in our Sunday School classes. The testimonies always took instant root in our hearts and we could not deny them. They became the compass in our souls that directed us back to the God of miracles, the God who always shows up, the God who is faithful in all areas of our lives, no matter the circumstance.[58]

Our parents and even our grandfather, Amos Neptune, constantly pulled us into their conversations of wonders, miracles and testimonies outside of church. They would summon us altogether and say "Listen to this! We have another Holy Spirit story for you." Often times, it would be over hearty meals. To this day, those times are some of the most treasured gems in all of our hearts.

DEAR TO YOUR HEART

My mom has long held dear in her heart to the Word in Isaiah 8:18 since we were small children. It boldly declares *"Behold, I and the children whom the Lord has given me are for signs and wonders in Israel from the Lord of hosts, who dwells on Mt. Zion."* Now, we have taken it as a declaration over the lives of our children and we invite you to do the same. We are called to raise fearless generations in the power and love of the Lord, Jesus Christ.

Psalm 78:5-7 announces *"...That they should teach them to their children, that the generation to come might know, even the children yet to be born, that they may arise and tell them to their children, that they should put their confidence in God and not forget the works of God...."* Can you fathom the tremendous impact of our children knowing and loving Daddy God and releasing Him to the world around them? Now, is the time!

The Lord loved David because of His heart after Him. In all things, whether 'failures' or 'wins', David remembered the Lord's sovereign faithfulness and turned to His goodness every time. David's "wins" in new situations resulted from the building blocks of testimonies that had revealed to Him the Lord's generous heart and miraculous provision. In Psalm 119:24 David says *"Your testimonies also are my delight and my counselors."*

In stewarding healing and miracles in children, always tell
testimonies and help them recall testimonies that the Lord
already performed in their lives. Edify our children in His
testimonies that they may become the fiber of their beings
and steward of their lives into the full reign of Heaven on
earth.[59]

A CULTURE OF TESTIMONY

We created a culture of treasuring and telling the testimony.
They were learning that God who performed crazy miracles
and provision, was doing it now through them and would
continue to do it with them. This stirred up so much
excitement, joy and thankfulness with the Lord. Parents
were telling me stories of their first graders trying to get
them to pray for strangers on the street, their kids healing
family members and friends at home and reports of the
fruit that was not only manifesting in their kiddos' lives, but
in their own hearts too. Some of the parents in tears of
thankfulness, told me that whatever I was doing with their
kids created so much passion and expectancy with the Lord
that they would have never thought possible for their child
so young.

My students from this conservative Christian school saw
everything from headaches, colds, bumps and bruises, hurt
feelings healed to symptoms of attention and hyperactivity
disorders, limbs growing out and people raised from the
dead. Years passed, and I am still hearing testimonies of

those students and how God is working through them as a result of that first year. Thank You Jesus!

STEP OUT ON HIS STORY

The testimonies bring life instead of death.[60] David worshipped the Lord with His heart with the intimate, ever-growing knowing that the Lord is good all of the time. Remembering the testimony, births confidence in who He says He is and ignites an expectation for God to perform His Word.[61]

Throughout the amazing historical stories of David in the Bible, He is always basing his future success on the Lord's faithful providence in his life. *"I considered my ways and turned my feet to Your testimonies."* *Psalm 119:59* When presented with any foreseeable unknown, children will know the direction to walk in based on the testimonies stored up in their hearts and minds.

> *Remembering the testimony, births confidence in who He says He is and ignites an expectation for God to perform His Word.*

JESUS ALIVE IN US

The Ark of the Covenant, also known as the Ark of the Testimony, is a prophetic picture to the New Testament church that began on the day of Jesus' resurrection and release of the Holy Spirit. It highlights how God's Presence is with His people wherever we go and His Testimony is our testimony.[62] We carry the Presence of the Living God, His story continues to take place in our lives. Wherever we go and whatever we do, He is with us and miracles happen.

This past year, was a year of back and forth between great glory and tough trials. Through it all, His Peace was constant and we continued to act based on His Truth instead of what we were experiencing. I felt a little worn out through it all and I was talking to God about it. Throughout my contemplation with Him, I told him I couldn't describe how I fully felt and instantly, a picture popped into my head. I saw something being squeezed in a vice with oil streaming out of it. The picture prompted me to recall the verse about being hard-pressed, so, I looked it up and was blown away by what I read.

2 Corinthians 4:7-11 reads "But we have this treasure in earthen vessels that the excellence of the power may be of God and not of us. We are hard-pressed on every side, yet not crushed; we are perplexed, but not in despair; persecuted, but not forsaken; struck down, but not destroyed— always carrying about in the body the dying of the Lord Jesus, that the life of Jesus also may be manifested in our body. For we who live are always delivered to death for Jesus' sake, that the life of Jesus also may be manifested in our mortal flesh."

The bottom line is that we are living testimonies of the Living Testimony. Death may show its face, but Life is the final Answer!

We are designed to be testimonies of His glory. All that was paid for is continuing to be made manifest through us and His story of Life is always the beautiful finisher. *"The thief comes only to steal and kill and destroy; I came that they may have life and have it to the full." John 10:10*

TESTIMONY OF LIFE IN US

Following this revelatory account during the summer of July 2016, I started to have unusual sharp pains in my body, nausea and vomiting, followed by an abnormally heavy menstrual cycle. I started to research my symptoms online and concluded that it must be some type of ovarian cyst. I also read that taking an at home pregnancy test would usually read positive with a cyst and so I took one. The results were positive. I knew it had to be a cyst! In my mind, I was definitely not pregnant as I had been on medication to prevent it. So, I called in to schedule an appointment with my obstetrician to get a proper diagnosis and treatment. Meantime, I had two of my closest friends Allyson and Sarah, praying for me.

The office was full, but due to my concerning symptoms, they were able to squeeze me in with one of their physician's assistants. Upon the usual initial visit of leaving a urine sample, it was officially determined that I was nothing short of pregnant. The PA listened to my symptoms and did an ultrasound to try and determine what was happening with the baby inside my womb. She had difficulty being able to make out what was happening, so, she scheduled me for higher resolution ultrasound services and blood work done every other day at a lab. I was requested to come back to their office the following week to discuss my results with both the physician's assistant and my obstetrician. Before leaving the room, she prayed over me.

I went in for my scheduled appointment for the advanced imaging ultrasound. The tech was using a real-time sonography and taking multiplanar sonographic images. The tech was not authorized to share her findings in full with me at the time, but sent my results over to my obstetrician to be discussed. However, she did plainly tell me that it was a non-developing fetus and it did not have a heartbeat. These were her findings as recorded in the appendices of this book: no definite fetal pole identified, a yolk sac present but no amnion and no fetal heartbeat (see appendix).

During this time, I was going in for my seventy-two hour lab work to monitor my hCG pregnancy hormone levels through periodic blood draws. Upon the initial lab work being completed, I received a phone call from my women's health office telling me that my results showed my hCG levels rapidly dropping instead of doubling and that I was definitely having a miscarriage.

I broke down in tears. I was a mix of emotions. I recently had close family members who experienced a tragic miscarriage during their first pregnancy. I had clung on to the Lord right beside them as they and others prayed in faith for the baby to come alive throughout the course of a couple weeks. Yet, the baby never revived on this earth. Part of me was feeling relieved that I would not be having my fourth child while they had yet to have their first. The other part of me cried out in anguish for the failing news of this precious baby that I wanted with all of my heart.

At the time, I did not want anyone else to know what was happening. In confidence, I only told my husband Jon, my parents and my two best friends. The moment I started to tell my mom, she slapped her hand across my womb and abruptly declared with an authoritative overhaul of fiery boldness and unwavering decree "There is absolutely no way, this baby will die!" A second of silence followed. Then, my parents and I, laughed at the powerful verdict that had risen up from her spirit, without thinking. My dad boldly joined in and they continued to pray over my womb, rebuking death and releasing life! My parents and my husband, each prayed for life over my womb. That night, I declared life over our little baby too. Despite the negative report from the advanced imaging services and the medically confirmed reports of my hormonal levels rapidly dropping, I hadn't had any more bleeding or odd accompanying symptoms after prayer.

At my follow-up appointment while waiting for the doctors to come in, I placed my hands on my womb and said "Lord, I want this baby." Shortly after, the doctors came into the room to go over my ultrasound images and lab work.

My doctor said "Well, this is definitely a miscarriage."

I started to fight back tears that were seemingly impossible to dam up. Small trickles made their way down my cheeks. I took a deep breath and pressed my lips together to regain composure as I listened to her continue on.

She relayed to me how my hormone levels not only had dropped the usual falling levels during a seventy-two hour period to indicate a definite miscarriage, but that my ultrasound images showed the baby dead with no heartbeat. The baby measured smaller than what it should have been measuring and the sac around it was collapsed.

At the unfortunate news, the floodgates of my sadness unleashed and I couldn't help but cry in front of both of the women. The doctor continued on talking about the different options for miscarriages, so, I could be aware of what to expect.

Not long after, she wanted to check me on the ultrasound to see where the lifeless baby was at in terms of leaving my womb. I calmed down and laid back as she began to look at my womb through the ultrasound. After a few seconds, she began to exclaim "Oh my gosh! Heike, come here!" Both ladies looked at the screen intently, the PA baffled, the doctor all smiles. "Do you see this?" said Jenne, my obstetrician. "Everything is perfect and there is a heartbeat!"

"What do you think happened?" exclaimed Heike.

"It's our first miracle" Jenne exclaimed! Both ladies rejoiced. I was in shock!

She measured the fetus through the ultrasound. My obstetrician recorded that there was no cardiac activity the previous week, measuring at six weeks while this time, the baby was measuring at nine weeks and four days! We listened for and heard a strong heartbeat at one hundred seventy-one beats per minute. Life conquered the grave! God raised the dead again! And this time, it was inside my own body!

Both doctors were ecstatic! I apologized for my shock with a slight laugh, utterly amazed at the miraculous turn of events. I was just bawling at the news of death moments ago and now bewildered at the immediate turnaround, trumpeting a celebration of life!

We finished up our conversation and both of the doctors began to pray, giving thanks to God. Once they left the room. I got dressed and opened the door to head towards the front of the office to schedule follow-up appointments. I passed a group of female doctors, nurses and office administrators all huddled around my obstetrician to hear the account of their first miracle at their practice. This astounding resurrection was something that they had been contending to see in their office for quite some time. All mouths hung open, eyes wide with amazement, they turned to look at me as I was walking out. I gave a sheepish smile and headed out the door to the front office administrators.

> *Life conquered the grave! God raised the dead again! And this time, it was inside my own body!*

"Aren't you so happy?" asked the lady who was checking me out and setting me up with my next appointments.

"I am amazed!" I replied. She smiled, congratulated me and sent me on my way with my next steps in hand.

Wow God, you are amazing. I thought to myself as I got in my car. Right away, I called my husband and then my parents to share the news. Then, I put my hands on my womb and spoke to the tiny baby that was growing inside. *I'm so happy you're alive and I can't wait to meet you.*

The whole drive home, I pondered at His Greatness and wondered what this little baby might be like. The previous revelations and verses about being designed to carry the resurrection life of Jesus burned in my heart and mind.[63] *Death may show its face, but Life is the final Answer!*

Every following checkup thereafter was flawless; a miracle of life, medically documented (see appendix). A dead miscarrying baby to an alive, full-term carrying baby. Our fourth child, Emma, born March 15, 2017. Praise be to God!

HIS PRESENCE ALIVE IN US

We are carriers of His Presence and literally walk in the way of the cross.[64] We have unlimited access vertically to Him and we have unlimited freedom horizontally to display His glory to the world around us.[65] We behold the mandate that we'll see an exponential increase of what Jesus paid for on the cross because His increase lives in us.[66] It's our honor and our glory to behold it.[67] Thank You Jesus!

Place a high value on cultivating an expectancy and awareness of His Presence at work and wonder in your children's everyday lives. It is quite easy to do and actually stirs up great excitement and wonder in your children. It builds up the spiritual muscles: that nothing is impossible with God, it's already been bought and paid for and His Kingdom made manifest is easy because we just are the open conduits for His Grace to flow through us. I practiced these values with my second grade and first grade classes when I taught at a Christian school.

There was always a focus on what He was doing in the moment and promised to do and we saw God show up every time.

During Bible time, I would always tell a testimony that fit with the Bible story we were talking about. I would say "God was, is and always will be. Does that mean what God did, He is doing on the earth right now and He will continue to do it again?" My students would always reply with a resounding *"yes"*. I would continue on and ask them the rhetorical question that if God said we would do these things and even greater things than Jesus did, would we? Then, whenever someone was upset or hurt I would always ask for volunteers to pray. There was always a focus on what He was doing in the moment and promised to do and we saw God show up every time.[68]

MIRACLES HAPPEN WHILE LOOKING AT HIM

Not only does healing happen in our family, but miracles that make you wonder too. We just bought each of our boys an expensive airplane set for Christmas. The characters that came with the airplane were only available through this special set. Both of our boys played with their airplanes constantly and brought them with them wherever they went in the house.

On one occasion, Noah insisted that he hold one of his small guys with him while he was going potty. Despite Jon's no, Noah took it with him and accidentally dropped and flushed him down the toilet. Noah started to panic, bawling at the loss of his new toy. When his tears stopped, we prayed and tried the plunger. Nothing.

Truthfully, we thought it was a lesson well learned. We definitely weren't going to buy this brand new, expensive set just so he could have this particular guy. Despite my husband and my persistent no's to his request, Noah confidently said "Daddy God will get me one in Jesus' name."

Two weeks passed, and we were in the playroom with the kids. Right in the middle of the toy-free floor was Noah's lost guy! We were all stunned. We had all witnessed this toy's forever disappearance and strangely, there he was! "Noah Look!" we exclaimed.

Noah picked him up and looked him over. "Jesus got him for me?" Noah asked bewildered.

"Yes!" we responded in awe and wonder.

"Did He use a helicopter and go get him out of the potty?" he asked logically.

"We don't know how He did it, but Jesus must love you very much!" we responded.

"Yes, He does" said Noah with a smile on his face.

When nurturing belief in God to perform the miraculous, there are no nos, only I don't knows. *Psalm 147:5 "Great is our Lord, and mighty in power; His understanding is infinite."*

When nurturing belief in God to perform the miraculous, there are no nos, only I don't knows.

Whether it's a how He does something or why He doesn't do something at a point within our time frame, the honest "I don't know" response places an awe and an awareness that God is bigger than us. He is who He says He is and He does what He says He does. He is the God of the impossible! *Luke 1:37 says "For with God, nothing will be impossible."*

This is the Truth we stand upon. This is the God we serve. This response creates an expectancy on His very nature and being, Truth, and nurtures a relationship of ever growing hope and faithfulness with our Lord and Savior.[69] Our eyes remain looking to Him. Our posture remains open, yielded to His Majesty. Our journey continues onward with the Great I Am.

BELIEVE IN HIM

In the Old Testament, Moses performed great and mighty deeds with God because He knew the ways of royalty. Moses knew that everything a royal decreed, was carried out. If he was good for his word, then surely the Word of the Living God was good. Astounding miracles happened through Moses because He acted upon the Lord's decree. Mighty and marvelous signs and wonders were accomplished as a result. Jesus, performed miracles based on the nature and faithfulness of God too.

The testimonies of God, testify of His Grace.

In Mark 9, a father brings a boy to Jesus who has a demon. The boy is wallowing and foaming at the mouth. The father asks Jesus to heal if He is able. In verse 23, Jesus replies *"If you can? All things are possible to him who believe."* Believe in this verse is the Greek word *pisteuō* which means to have confidence in someone; to credit.[70] The foundation of miracles laid out by Jesus saying that they are a fruit of one's confidence in Daddy God's trustworthiness. The testimonies of God, testify of His Grace.

If you have confidence in God, He will show up. As God shows up, record what He does.[71] It is a faith builder for those who know Him and a faith starter for those who are now invited into a relationship with God.[72] Treasure and tell the testimony.[73] Remind children of His faithful hand in their lives. You are building monuments that change history in the lives of young children and those around the world.

We hear about the great men and women of faith. Now, is the time to hear about the great children of faith![74] People from all over the world will come to Jesus because they will hear, see and know that these are the people of God for even their children are blessed. Hallelujah!

PONDER THE POSSIBILITIES

Reflect on your history with the Lord. Write down events in your life where God faithfully showed up. These are landmarks in your life of His faithfulness.

Ask God to give you a picture or words of His faithfulness towards you and your children. What comes to mind?

Now, ask God to give you a picture or words for you and your children as you continually step out with Him in your future. Record it.

PROCLAIM

I and my children are for signs and wonders.

History, "His story" is taking shape in my life.

I have access to all of Him, always.

I have full freedom to display Him.

There are no nos, only I don't knows.

I am a living testimony.

I am from God and God always shows up.

I am open and yielded to what He wants to do.

Nothing is impossible with God.

My God is a God of miracles.

Life is the final answer.

BE FRUITFUL AND MULTIPLY

Actively tell testimonies with your children. Tell testimonies from the Bible and testimonies you have heard or witnessed since those biblical accounts.

Always remind your children of His faithfulness by turning their eyes to His testimonies by saying "If God did _____, will He do it again?" Yes!

When praying for others. Give thanks for every bit of breakthrough. Even if you happen to not witness anything in the physical, give thanks, for something is still happening in the spiritual.

Leave everyone around you expectantly looking for God even after you pray by telling the recipient of prayer to keep checking out their body part or looking for improvement in the areas that needed healed.

Always stay in Truth. If someone asks you for why something didn't happen, say "I don't know. God said (Truth verse). I am not moved by what I see, but by what I believe."

Chapter 5

C is for Celebrate

"We will rejoice in Your salvation,
And in the name of our God we will set up our banners!
May the Lord fulfill all your petitions."

Psalm 20:5

All throughout the Bible, people celebrated with great rejoicing proclaiming His name and marvelous, mighty deeds. Look and see what the Lord has done! He is who He says He is and He'll do what He says He'll do! Our banners are set up, firmly planted in the soil of His faithfulness and His Promises. Victory waves its glory and majesty over us, testifying to all the earth that Heaven is here.

David proclaims in *Psalm 145:1-7* *"I will extol You, my God, O King; And I will bless Your name forever and ever. Great is the Lord, and greatly to be praised; And His greatness is unsearchable. One generation shall praise Your works to another, And shall declare your mighty acts. I will meditate on the glorious splendor of Your majesty, And on Your wondrous works. Men shall speak of the might of Your awesome acts, And I will declare Your greatness. They shall utter the memory of Your great goodness, And shall sing of Your righteousness."* David's heart of celebration to the Father moved him to prosper in kingly rule and reign under the promises of God. His praise promoted promise and his posture prophesied position.

A culture of celebration is birthed out of treasuring and telling the testimony from one generation to another; praising His goodness which prospers our futures and brings all things into completion in His holy name.[75] Like Jesus riding into town on a donkey while people cheered him onwards, the Spirit of Revival rides in upon humanity in the atmosphere of praise.

1 Chronicles 16:9 says "Sing to Him, sing praises to Him; Speak of all His wonders." Praise is powerful. It trumpets His arrival, crashing down every stronghold, His glorious Kingdom instantaneously established. The shouts of His glory, leave enemy lines demolished and unlock mysteries for His believing beloved - full freedom at wondrous play. Praise victoriously waves His story. His nature compels Him to continuously act on that establishment of praise because His Word has been made known; a

> *... the Spirit of Revival rides in upon humanity in the atmosphere of praise.*

celebratory landmark of His Word made manifest.[76] The mere utterance of it, performs life; even dry bones must dance!

Throughout my teaching career, our celebratory conversations of His testimonies throughout the Bible and modern day events created such a fiery desire to see God actively move through them that it catapulted our class into practicing healing. Every time, I told them a testimony about Jesus, I would naturally extol His greatness and encourage my students that God would move the same way through them! Continual celebration of His testimonies through praise, generated surmounting swells in the spirits of my children that they just had to break forth in a tsunami of His Spirit! The students were overjoyed and all on board! "Miss Moore, can we please try it?"

"Okay…" I said. In my head I was thinking a lot of conflicting thoughts because I wasn't fully confident in praying for healing myself. Yet, I knew that Father wanted to teach them and would honor their desire and willingness to give it a try. So, we began to practice healing together.

"Okay, who needs healed?" A few hands shot up and I called on a boy named Aiden. I asked him what he wanted healed. Aiden matter of factly stated that he had one arm shorter than the other. He said he had it all of his life. My mouth hung open, my eyes wide. I had yet to see limbs grow out through my hands. I glanced at my students, joyful anticipation and adventure danced in their eyes.

"Alright, we will pray for you" I replied. I summoned everyone to the carpet where we usually gathered and got out a ruler. We measured both of his arms. One arm was a whole inch shorter than the other. We wrote down the number on a sticky note.

Then, I told everyone to put their hands on him and command his arm to grow. "1-2-3...go!" All of the children prayed at once. "Stop!" I said. We stopped and measured both arms. I couldn't help but laugh.

"What happened?" they exclaimed.

Laughing, I replied "both arms grew a half inch. They are both longer but the one is still a whole inch longer than the other!" Aiden's eyes were wide and joined in with laughter, followed by everyone else. "Let's put our hands on his longest arm and command it to go back and match the other arm. 1-2-3...Go!"

Once again, the children prayed. Then, we measured it and all of the kids eagerly waited for the results. "They're perfectly even!" I announced. Everyone cheered and clapped! Aiden shocked, my students victoriously celebrating! We were all greatly encouraged and eager to heal more people.

Stewarding conversations of testimonies, praising His name and encouraging one another compels us to step out and give it a go! Our eyes are focused on His faithfulness as we step out to practice and decree what He practiced and decreed. His glory is made manifest to those who believe.[77] Celebrating every breakthrough of His domain, snowballs into complete fruition as we persevere on His Truth. Keep our eyes on Him and as we walk, we will see heaven released.[78]

FEASTS AND THANKSGIVING

Exodus 12:14 pronounces *"So this day shall be to you a memorial, and you shall keep it as a feast to the Lord throughout your generations. You shall keep it as a feast by an everlasting ordinance."* The word feast in this passage is the Hebrew word *chagag*, which literally means celebrate.[79]

Testimonies are meant to be kept as reminders and feasted upon in celebration. If we don't celebrate the testimonies of God now, we won't be celebrating Him in our future. The opposite of the word celebration is condemnation. So, a life without celebration is a life of condemnation and there is no future in that; literally![80]

> *... a life without celebration is a life of condemnation and there is no future in that; literally!*

Throughout His Word, God appointed people to set up celebratory feasts as historical landmarks. Two of the feasts He ordained and encouraged were the Feast of the First Fruits and the Feast of the Harvest.[81] They were to be a statute throughout the generations of His dwelling place.

We are to be a people who not only celebrate in harvest, but who also celebrate in the first fruits of it. If we can learn to celebrate the first fruits along with the harvest, we will continually see His Kingdom come through all of our labors with Him.[82]

When teaching children to heal, we always look to what God is doing in that moment and partner with it. We generate excitement and expectancy for God to show up based on His testimonies. For example, Kennedy and Mariah, prayed for a fellow classmate commanding pain to go and that Arthur's arm would feel all better. They asked how he was doing. His response was that it still hurt. "Okay, thank You Jesus. Let's pray again" the girls said without hesitation. Then, Kennedy and Mariah, prayed again.

When teaching children to heal, we always look to what God is doing in that moment and partner with it.

"Do you feel better now?"

"Yes, I can move it all around, thank you" Arthur happily replied.

These six and seven-year-old girls not only prayed authoritatively, but they recognized the first fruits of what God was doing, gave thanks for it and prayed again.

Our two sons, ages two and three, just got into the bathtub. It was just starting the process of being filled up when all of a sudden, the water pressure rapidly declined. The water went from sputtering to nothing. Both boys were disappointed, especially, our eldest son Noah. He definitely let us know that he wasn't okay with what happened through his whining and complaining. I told him "Noah remember how we just read about Jesus praying and calming the water during the storm?" He stopped and just looked at me. "Pray for the water."

He put his hands on the faucet and looked at me. I repeated myself "pray for the water to come."

He said "water go in Jesus' name, amen." Nothing happened. He said "It didn't work."

I told him to pray again. So, he did. "Look!" he said, "It's working!"

The tiniest stream of water came out of the faucet. He was instantly happy and went back to playing with the water he had. To me, it was just a little more than a drip, but I didn't say anything except "Thank you Daddy God. Noah, that was awesome!"

How we choose to position ourselves in our current situation usually determines how our next opportunity for breakthrough will turnout.

The next time we encountered another obstacle, I reminded Noah of how he prayed for the water and how God showed up. So, he was able to pray in confidence for the next need. Usually we saw an immediate answer and provision as a result.

How we choose to position ourselves in our current situation usually determines how our next opportunity for breakthrough will turnout. Regardless of the outcome, always celebrate God's goodness and what He is doing in the moment.[83] If we can see who He is through His testimonies before we pray, then as we pray, we will see Him perform another great work!

If we give thanks for what He is doing, we will see what He'll accomplish.[84]

As children continually practice healing in this manner, they will see more than they can begin to ask or imagine.[85] Feasting on His Word, keeping our eyes fixed on Him, giving thanks for what He is doing and remaining open to what He wants to do is also how the miraculous pours out through His believing beloved.[86]

ENCOURAGEMENT

It is of no coincidence that Jesus' first miracle recorded in the Bible is of His turning water into wine at a wedding celebration where the initial, natural supply ran out. Not only that, His supernatural supply was the very best! The wedding celebration is a picture of what we have entered into as a New Covenant church where the body is His Bride, drinking the 'New Wine' and He is the Bridegroom, pouring it out!

If we give thanks for what He is doing, we will see what He'll accomplish.

When we are in right relationship with each other, unified in Spirit, cross-denominationally and can celebrate each other and His testimonies in our lives, more of His Presence than we can contain will be poured out upon His people.[87] The overflow will touch others and more people will enter into His Kingdom. Celebrating brings unity and empowers a move of God among His people. There is no hierarchy. It's us with Him. We are one in Christ!

When championing healing and miracles in our children, it is important to create a culture of celebration. To be excited together about what He has done, what He is doing and what He is going to do. To rejoice together, valuing each child as powerful, loved and apart of the miraculous work that God is doing.

Position yourself as a cheerleader. Cheerleaders at a football game promote their team win or lose. They continually generate an atmosphere of encouragement and enthusiasm to cheer their team onward into success.

In Deuteronomy 3:28, God tells Moses to strengthen and encourage Joshua for he was going to lead the children of Israel across the Jordan to inherit the Promised Land. Encouragement is necessary for people to successfully lead others into their inheritance and walk in the full promises of God. Encouragement fuels faith, sparking perseverance to finish its race.

Encouragement acts as the midwife for Heaven's destiny to be birthed into full fruition in a person's life.

The Lord says in 1 Corinthians 14:31 that He wishes *we would all prophesy one by one so that everyone may be encouraged.* People of every age are being called up in Christ to rightly rule and reign with Him. If we want people to attain the full measure of Christ to fully release Christ, we must encourage one another to get there.[88] Encouragement acts as the midwife for Heaven's destiny to be birthed into full fruition in a person's life.

Currently, masses of people of our time are questioning our nation's original values of freedom, questioning their own identities and worth and the Bride is being shaken awake because there is an unsettling that doesn't line up with our value system of Heaven. There is a recognition of what needs to be done and encouragement is needed to bring it into fruition. The more we encourage one another, the more coals will be added to the steam engine of revival that will rapidly accelerate and cover more territory than we ever thought possible.

COACHES OF THE FAITH

Our roles are to be like cheerleaders who continually encourage their team to reach the goal line and to be like great coaches who continually look for opportunities to practice our faith.[89] When reviewing the stories of football coaches who were inducted into the Hall of Fame, I came across common values that made them triumphant in their coaching careers. A few of the common threads mentioned are that they:

- weren't afraid
- empowered others
- stewarded the seasons they were in
- believed in miracles
- knew how to remain focused under pressure
- never settled
- knew how to build from the ground up

We must be fearless believers of God who empower others, steward the seasons that we are in, believe in the miraculous, know how to remain focused under pressure and persevere in all things.[90] We do not let the lack we are experiencing to waiver our position in His Word and leave us unprepared for the next assignment. We remain open and yielded to the God of Miracles who has an unending supply to pour out.

If we teach and champion our children in this way so that their eyes are always shifted off of the problem and onto the Solution, Victory will make itself known in the history books.[91] We glorify Him in what He has done and what He will do and marvel at His awesome deeds.

Remind your children of the testimonies, build them up, and encourage them as they practice them. Champion them through celebrating God at work and God in them. Have fun and be amazed! You and the children whom the Lord has given you are for signs and wonders!

> *If we teach and champion our children in this way so that their eyes are always shifted off of the problem and onto the Solution, Victory will make itself known in the history books.*

It doesn't matter if you have shy and quiet children. It doesn't matter if you have skeptical children. You keep these core Kingdom values, encourage them and practice them and everyone will eventually flourish in them. *"Retain the standard of sound words which you have heard from me, in the faith and love which are in Christ Jesus. Guard, through the Holy Spirit who dwells in us, the treasure which has been entrusted to you." 2 Timothy 1:13-14* The shyest, quietest, most skeptical child in my first grade classroom prayed to raise the dead the first time he stepped out. Don't give up! Focus on what He's doing and rejoice in it!

PONDER THE POSSIBILITIES

God has given us Good News of great joy to partake in and share with those around us. Why is celebration so important in the Kingdom of God?

The antonym of celebration is condemnation. Why is it important to champion a practice of celebration in our daily lives?

Ask God to show you ways to honor and celebrate others. Model it and encourage it in your children. What does this look like?

When we are unable to celebrate someone or something, we need to forgive and repent. Repentance and forgiveness are powerful tools that restore us to full freedom and right Kingdom standing. What is the impact of modeling and practicing repentance and forgiveness with our children? How do they benefit from it?

PROCLAIM

I lift up Your name O God! I will bless it forever!

I celebrate all that You have done!

I celebrate all that You will do!

I tell nations of what You have done!

Great are You Lord and greatly to be praised!

I declare your acts and meditate on Your splendor and wonder.

I celebrate you with my children.

You celebrate and rejoice over me!

I celebrate and encourage others.

I keep my eyes on You and look to what You are doing!

I always give thanks to my God.

I praise You forever and stand on Your Word.

BE FRUITFUL AND MULTIPLY

When stepping out to pray, remind one another of His testimonies. Share a testimony with the person who you are about to pray for. This draws our eyes to focus on the Faithful One.

Example: *God always takes pain away. He just healed a lady of shoulder pain. May I pray for the pain in your neck to go?*

After you pray for healing, ask the person to check it out. Can he or she do something that they weren't able to do before? Ask them what their pain level is now.

Celebrate by giving thanks. Giving thanks keeps our eyes focused on what He's doing and leaves everyone open to what He is about to do again. Pray again if needed. Leave everyone with their eyes on Jesus.

Anytime you or someone else steps out to pray, give words of encouragement, high fives, etc. Encourage and celebrate everyone's attempts for giving it a go! Encouragement propels people into their destinies.

Chapter 6

Purposely Powerful

"In Him also we have obtained an inheritance,
being predestined according to the purpose of Him
who works all things according to the counsel of His will,
that we who first trusted in Christ should be to the praise of His glory."

Ephesians 1:11-12

T hrough all of the different ways the Kingdom manifests throughout the Bible, it is clear that there are no formulas or rules as to how to perform them. The bottom line is, Kingdom operates on the substance, the person of Christ.[92] Believing Jesus Ministries says "Faith is confidence in Him. Confidence in His good character and His good nature to perform what He said He would" through you! Do you believe what He said? It's Truth!

It's fascinating to think that His Kingdom is so vast yet meant to be displayed through the unique beauty of His children. When we ponder at the awe and wonder of His glory that who are we that He would be mindful of us, we are cultivating a worshipful heart that invites the heart of the Father. *"He is your praise and He is your God, who has done these great and awesome things for you which your eyes have seen." Deuteronomy 10:21*

A HEART LIKE DAVID

It was David as a young boy who was entrusted to look after his father's sheep, protecting them from lions and bears. He traveled to the battle lines to supply his brothers with food and rose up with confidence to defeat the Philistine giant, Goliath, who was widely known war hero and victoriously conquered him in the name of the Lord of Hosts, winning a battle for a nation. He was soon summoned to serve as the king's armor bearer and found favor with Him. Eventually, he would become king himself.

Renowned by God in the Bible for his worshipful heart, David was a King with incredible conquests who changed history.[93] He pondered on the Lord often, marveling at His Majesty. In God Almighty, He recognized great love and faithfulness and personally invited God into His life's journey. David glorified God by thanking and praising Him, looking to Him as the answer to any obstacle or enemy that sprung from the shadows. God was there to be a part of His every day. He recognized it and He utilized it.

David made God personal in his life beginning in his childhood. It's through David's line that Jesus made all of God personally available to us. It's the positioning of our heart and mind, the stewarding of putting it into practice that brings more of the Kingdom. If you are not using what you have, why get more?

> *It's the positioning of our heart and mind, the stewarding of putting it into practice that brings more of the Kingdom.*

In Psalm 26:3, David says "For your loving kindness is before my eyes, and I have walked in Your truth." Truth in this passage is the Hebrew word *'emeth*, also meaning faithfulness.[94] The Lord's loving kindness and faithfulness marked David in his youth, serving as the steam engine of revival into adulthood; the surmounting greatness of God at work in his life unfolding from his childlike trust and expectancy. David remained open to the God of all things are possible and thus co-created a profound life of love, honor, adventure, strength, friendship and promise. David powerfully reigned with God all throughout his life, his favor and influence always increasing as he journeyed from faith to faith with the King of kings. This is God's loving heart and purpose for all of His royal children. *"The grace of the Lord Jesus Christ, and the love of God, and the fellowship of the Holy Spirit, be with you all." 2 Corinthians 13:14*

MOVING FREELY IN LOVE

We are stewards of our children's hearts and though at times they are unable to see what they truly need, they have a pretty good way of communicating they are in need of something. That something is found in Jesus, our hope secure in the being of Love.[95] When children are growing up in an environment that is grounded and rooted in love, they have complete freedom to be themselves; displaying Christ naturally in whatever they do. As they freely move in Him, they freely release the Father to those around them.

Playfulness is a term that embraces freely moving about in enjoyment and satisfaction. Jesus loves to manifests His Kingdom through His kids even in their play. Playing with God is powerful because it freely allows Holy Spirit to move through the unique expression of His children.[96] Playing awakens a childlike mentality. When you learn to release Holy Spirit as you play with Him, others will be healed and touched by His Presence.

Our son Noah ran his knee into the corner of his train table painfully hard and came as fast as he was able to towards me, bawling. I was in the middle of making him a peanut butter sandwich. I heard what happened and I had this confidence in me that I knew that his tears were about to completely stop. *Jesus will heal this, no problem was my thought.* Without really thinking about what I was doing, I slapped some peanut butter on it. His whole body jolted. He stopped crying and looked at me in unexpected shock! I took one, quick lick, the pain left, he laughed and ran off.

There is no formula in this as to how to heal as there are no formulas in healing. There is only a bottom line and that bottom line is Jesus Christ.[97] He is our firm foundation, the Author and Perfector of our faith. He is the Standard upon which we heal and the right we have to practice it. He moves on our words because He is the Word. When we declare Him, we release Him. *"For truly I say to you to you, if you have faith the size of a mustard seed, you will say to this mountain, 'Move from here to there,' and it will move; and nothing will be impossible for you." Matthew 17:20*

> *...God will move on behalf of our authority every time, but He'll also move through our free expressions because we are the very carriers of His Presence.*

Jesus illustrated some playfulness in the healing of the blind man. He spit in the mud and put it on the blind man's eyes. *Wash your eyes and show yourself to the High Priest,* Jesus said. There is much more revelation to be discovered in this story but it is a testimony that so easily unravels our minds. The miracle is recorded after numerous accounts of Jesus healing people authoritatively through commands. It was as if He was showing us that yes, God will move on behalf of our authority every time, but He'll also move through our free expressions because we are the very carriers of His Presence. Love delights in us simply as we move and breathe and as we move and breathe in Him, we'll release Love wherever we go.[98]

Knowing that we are legally part of the solution and beholding the knowledge that God will move through us in unexpected ways, is fun and encouraging. It puts the awe and wonder back on Jesus. Before I journeyed into healing, I met a little girl who felt led to dance over a woman who was laying on the floor with stage 4 cancer. As the girl gracefully swooped her arm over the woman, the woman felt a surge of power go through her body. She felt like she might be healed and after a thorough examination from her doctor, she was! It was in the girl's joyful freedom of dance before the Lord that healed the woman on her deathbed.

"Now may the God of hope fill you with all joy and peace in believing, so that you will abound in hope by the power of the Holy Spirit." Romans 15:13

Love delights in us simply as we move and breathe and as we move and breathe in Him, we'll release love wherever we go.

THE CALL IN LOVE

When we begin to taste and see the splendor and the glory of the Lord, how fascinating our lives become! Hope for the world is magnified, Love personified through the lives of those that believe. If we can be childlike to receive His Grace and childlike in our display of it, then we will see greater works than we could even begin to dream. The world needs Jesus. He is the Desire of the Nations and all of creation is groaning out for Him.[99] The world is waiting for Jesus to be revealed in every person of every age who believes in Him.[100]

Look at your hands. Your fingerprints are telltale signs that no one else is like you or will be like you. In the heart of your cells, you are marked by a cross-like glue, Laminin that holds things altogether. You are marked by Him in unique beauty, held together by His Word and born for such a time as this! [101] His Presence fills your temple. Freely you've received, freely give until the glory of the Lord fills the earth.[102] Hallelujah!

PONDERING THE POSSIBILITIES

Spend time in God's Presence. Ponder at the greatness of His Kingdom meant to be displayed through you. What do you feel? Hear? See? Smell? Experience? Etc.

Invite your children to spend time with God in this way with you. Trembling and glorying are both normal, biblical responses to the Presence and Kingdom of God. Enjoy!

How are you and your children purposed to know and grow with God? Why?

How do you cultivate being a son/daughter after His own heart?

How is He already pleased with you? Ask Him to show you His pleasure in you while spending time in His Presence.

PROCLAIM

I am born again for such a time as this!

I am meant to display Christ to the nations.

Love delights in me as I move and breathe.

People may never know God unless I allow myself to be a part of the solution that reveals Him to the people around me.

I have full confidence in His character. Therefore, I have a lot of faith.

My faith trumps any unbelief.

Freely I've received, freely I give.

When I declare Jesus, I release Jesus.

Jesus is the Desire of All Nations. People want Jesus and I've got Jesus to give them.

I grow in favor with God and man as I practice displaying Him wherever I go.

When I move, He moves.

He moves on my authority and He moves in my playfulness.

BE FRUITFUL AND MULTIPLY

Courageously start to step out in sharing God's Kingdom with people as you go about your day. As you see a need, step out to give what you've got. Invite your children to do so as well.

Examples:

- Someone is thirsty, fill their cup.
- Someone needs physical assistance. Help them. Take it a step further and ask if you may pray for them.
- Ask God for a creative way that He wants to heal someone. Try it. What happens?

Always bless and encourage the people you serve.

Chapter 7

Revival with Children

"Therefore you shall lay up these words of mine in your heart and in your soul, and bind them as a sign on your hand, and they shall be as frontlets between your eyes. You shall teach them to your children, speaking of them when you sit in your house, when you walk by the way, when you lie down, and when you rise up. And you shall write them on the doorposts of your house and on your gates, that your days and the days of your children may be multiplied... Every place on which the sole of your foot treads shall be yours... No man shall be able to stand against you..."

Deuteronomy 11:18-25

N ow is the time for this generation young and old to take hold of what was given to us through God's Son, Jesus Christ. All throughout the Old Testament, children are mentioned over and over again. Clear themes, reminding His children about the importance of remembering the testimony, treasuring God's Word in their hearts, expecting God to show up, taking hold of what He's promised and stepping into what He's given them are found all throughout it.

Jesus comes in the New Testament and all that has been made available is revealed. He calls and commissions us as sons and daughters, co-heirs with Christ to release the Kingdom wherever we go.[103] As we search out His mysteries, we discover that the impossible is now completely possible because Heaven invades earth through us.[104]

Jesus tells us in the Gospels to come into His Kingdom as children. Kids believing Jesus will have right relationships, live wisely and worship in Spirit and Truth. They will know His Presence, hear His voice, behold the testimony, heal the sick, raise the dead, release freedom to those around them, expect the impossible to become possible and overflow with the love of God and the fruit of His Spirit. It all begins with positioning ourselves to know the face of God and acting on His faithfulness.[105]

Peter, who at times was a timid man, successfully stepped out every time He looked to Jesus and remained focused on His face. Peter's name means *stone* and it was the name given to Him by God. God didn't see him as a timid man, but a solid man whose eyes remained focused on Him; a rock. This is how God see us! In His Word, He calls us living stones.[106] Stones that mark His Living Testimony. Stones that defeat giants in one, solid shot.

He calls us living stones. Stones that mark His Living Testimony. Stones that defeat giants in one, solid shot.

We are God's surprise weapon, allowing Victory to take up residence in the people and in the land through our active trust in the One True God.[107] The size of the rock doesn't matter, it is the size of our God that matters. In Christ, both children and adults are living stones. It is our responsibility and our honor, to train our children in the inheritances of Heaven; championing them in both the pastures and in the battlefield. If you personally feel ill equipped to lead children into their rightful reign and rule, simply open up what's possible for them and let them sling you into Heaven alongside them as they fearlessly step out to know, practice and perform the works of Jesus.

Step into this great adventure with a childlike heart. Exercise your authority in Him. Treasure and tell the testimony. Celebrate His faithfulness with endless possibilities. Sharpen and cheer each other into more of Heaven.[108] What a glorious day we live in with the Glorious One!

RESTORATION THROUGH CHILDLIKENESS

Mary modeled laying up the words of the Lord in her heart and soul. She pondered and marveled on them. The Lord chose her purity, delight and trust in Him, to birth the Prince of Peace; a heritage to all the world through the fruit of her womb. What marks the beginning of an ever-growing revival birthed through His people who trust and delight in Him? The ever resounding *yes* to our miraculous King, whose plans are so profound and worthy, our hearts and minds can only muse at its greatness but feel compelled to go forth, carrying His word and letting it come to fruition! *"For all the promises of God in Him are Yes, and in Him Amen, to the glory of God through us."*
1 Corinthians 1:20

A simple knowing of the true Gospel, awakens an eager appetite for more of the knowledge and Presence of the Living God. The more we taste, the more we see; the more ravenous our spirit becomes for His Kingdom manifest in the world around us through our very hands and feet.[109] Our hearts cry out *Oh Choose me!* Our Living God says *I have chosen you.* The possibilities at hand are limitless! [109] His glory is everlasting; surmounting on the promise and praise of His people. *Colossians 1:26-27* boldly proclaims *"The mystery that has been kept hidden for ages and generations, but is now disclosed to the Lord's people. To them God has chosen to make known among the Gentiles the glorious riches of this mystery, which is Christ in you, the hope of Glory."*

Revival is spreading throughout the world through believers in childlike faith who accept His Word and allow it to birth in their hearts and mind. Revival came into this world as a small child and it's through His children, that revival gains momentum, growing and multiplying throughout the earth. In Webster's Dictionary, one of the definitions for the world revival is the restoration of force, validity or effect. The restoration of force and validity came when the Covenant was made as Jesus' blood was poured out for many through His death and resurrection. *"For a covenant is valid only when men are dead, for it is never in force, while the one who made it lives."* *Hebrews 9:17*

> *Children are waiting to know what they have been destined and authorized to carry.*

For full reconciliation upon this earth, we need to embrace His Word and run with it! Revival is here and is rippling across the earth as His children are taking hold of His Word, naturally releasing Jesus to the world around them. The harvest is plentiful! All of His children, are already fully equipped and fully backed to get the job done.

Lay up what you've seen Him say and do in His Word throughout the living testimonies of His people and teach them to your children. Ponder His Word, practicing His Kingdom together. Encourage your children to finish the race marked out for them. Children are waiting to know what they have been destined and authorized to carry. They are always ready to run with what's been given to them. Children know they can change the world.

POWER IN TRAINING CHILDREN

Proverbs 22:6 instructs "Train up a child in the way he should go and when he is old he will not depart from it." The word go in this passage is a Hebrew noun, *peh*, meaning mouth. If children are exercising their authority, belief and celebration through their mouth, they are learning that His Truth proves true and acts in accordance with His Word made manifest through them. Upon their very breath and body, the Spirit moves.[110]

Solomon also says that *from the heart the mouth speaks.*[111] So, it is imperative to get the nature and character of the Word, Jesus Christ, laid up in our hearts and minds which is revealed in His testimonies. Testimonies will direct us how to go and invite the reign of Heaven in everything that we do. Testimonies will also open doors that no man can shut. Celebrating all that He has done and promises to do, moves a people into an extraordinary future, changing the course of history. Even now, strength has already been established upon the mouths of babes. *"O Lord our Lord, How majestic is Your name in all the earth, who have displayed Your splendor above the heavens! From the mouths of infants and nursing babes You have established strength." Psalm 8:1-2* Together, linking arms from generation to generation, we will step into the Promise Land among the Great Harvest of souls for King Jesus.

KINGLY CHILDREN

Josiah, is a prophetic picture found in 2 Kings, of what it looks like for kingly children to rule and reign on earth. Crowned king at age nine, he restored the city to the kingdom through his tender heart and humbleness to the Lord. He rebuilt the temple of worship, rightly restored people's relationships and the way they lived. Josiah's leadership wiped out evil's influence and restored celebration all unto God. This is just but a taste of what is meant for our children to rule and reign in our day. Children's kingly rule, reinstates a Kingly reign; evil influences can stand no more.[112]

Ironically enough, Josiah's name in Hebrew is *Yo'shiyah,* which means Healed by Yah. As children rule and reign through their tender hearts and humbled posture, Heaven's reign will fully manifest in all areas of life, influence and government. The world will be healed through the authority of a child. The people once again will rejoice, the city restored and the nations blessed![113] Heaven has called the children, now let us bring them in our midst and run the race marked out for us together.

> *Children's kingly rule, reinstates a Kingly reign; evil influences can stand no more.*

CHILDREN WHO CHANGE THE WORLD

Today, it is easier to find written records of adults who have impacted the world around them versus children. It's not typical for our society to promote the accomplishments or cheer on the potential of children. Yet, if you look for it, you will find stories of countless children who have powerfully impacted our world both in history and in modern day. The ones who are more easily recognized in today's culture are usually child prodigies. There are also children who remarkably excelled in something as a result of their parents recognizing what their children carried and therefore, positioned them in strategic ways to prosper their giftings and expand their influence.

Historical figures that are still celebrated and studied today are people like Pablo Picasso, Blaise Pascal, Mozart, Shirley Temple and Anne Frank. Did you know that they were all mere children when they started to make giant marks upon the hearts and minds of mankind? Some of them were instantly admired whereas others were realized after the fact.

Pablo Picasso's simple pleasure of painting transformed his culture, leaving his truly unique fingerprint throughout the nations. His first famous work Picador, painted at age eight! Blaise Pascal's natural ease and fascination with mathematics led him to practice theorems which lead to the famous Pascal's Theorem at age sixteen! Pascal's Theorem would be taught throughout schools for generations to come.

Mozart wrote his first composition at age six. He composed over six hundred pieces by the time he was thirty-five years old. While his music has ever since been enjoyed by a wide audience, today it is being studied even more as his music is scientifically determined to have a positive impact on the cognitive part of the brain.

Shirley Temple's adorable, heartwarming personality lit up the stage; touching hearts across America. Her endearing character and excellent tap dancing skills celebrated the loveliness of children and childhood. Even now, watching her movies awakens a nostalgia for innocence and love.

Anne Frank's diary became famous after she died at the age of fifteen in a concentration camp. Her diary is one of the most widely read works throughout the world today. The pouring out of her hopes, fears, joys and hardships she expressed throughout her documented historical experience of the Holocaust, humanizes the course of events to every reader. Through her simplistic, raw diary, people can connect with both the fears in the atrocities and hopes in the possibilities. Anne's diary simultaneously cautions people of the pure evil of prejudice; highlighting its horrific effects on those it torments and kills and solicits a call to honor those who have greatly sacrificed their lives for our liberty.

There are even incredible accomplishments from children in our modern day. An eight year old from Korea was invited by the United States to study at NASA after solving a complex calculus problem on a television show in Japan. The potential for this child and the impact he's making is mind blowing! A fifteen-year-old boy, designed a low cost artificial leg with an ability for knee and ankle movement. His ingenuity has already improved the quality of life for those who have lost a limb, rippling out to positively impact the people who surround those grateful recipients. A young girl, belts an operatic melody, elevating her listeners into a tangible heavenly awe.

These are only a few highlights of influential children who powerfully impacted and continue to influence the world around them. These children carried a natural love or gifting that was encouraged by their caregivers, who provided their children opportunities to prosper in their area of delight and eventual expertise.

There is a call, as a people to keep our eyes open, recognizing God on something or someone. Then, we are called to call it forth and bring it into completion. In Isaiah 41, God says that He called the generations forth from the beginning! He says He's chosen us! He's with us! He will surely help us, strengthen and uphold us! God has given us success since the beginning. Our success is meant to draw people into His Kingdom. He says *"that they may see and recognize, and consider and gain insight as well, that the hand of the Lord has done this, and the Holy One of Israel has created it."* Look at your little one; you are looking at success. Look at yourself; you are looking at success. *"For I know the plans that I have for you' declares the Lord, 'plans for welfare and not for calamity to give you a future and a hope.'"* Jeremiah 29:11

Some of us naturally blossom and excel at that which we were born to do, unafraid to display the vulnerabilities of our unique expressions. Others are noted for an unusual talent, mentored and positioned for excellence. Then, there are those of us who burn with a conviction of purpose for something. It sets our gaze and we set ablaze. In all of these scenarios, prosperity reigns through open hearts and minds, coupled with perseverance to see it through.

Florence Nightingale simply ministered to those in need in her youth. It was in her obedience to her heart's prompting that awoke a desire to serve people and save lives. Florence decided that she wanted to become a nurse. Her parents forbade it. She ignored the opposition, pursuing the burning call in her heart. Florence, eventually became an effective nurse and saved lots of lives. During the Crimean War, she was summoned to gather a team to serve injured and fallen soldiers. When she arrived onto the scene, Florence noted the whole operation was in shambles. The people had little hope of survival. After her assessment, she thought *not on my watch* and set to work! Thousands of lives were saved, healthcare systems and government operations revolutionized; the duty of a nurse, became an honorable one. Florence not only burned brightly with the hope and conviction that she could make a difference! She believed she could turn the whole operation around in the right direction. People deemed Miss Nightingale as 'The Lady of the Lamp." At night with her lamp lit, she attended to those in need, while calling things to order that were in disarray. Florence Nightingale is now renowned as the pioneer of modern nursing; a museum in England honors her name.

EVERY CHILD DISPLAYS HIM

Every child is born with the DNA of Heaven flowing through their veins. Chosen by His name, destined to display His marvelous deeds, so, that all might come to know Him as Lord and Savior, Father and Friend.[114] *"Who desires all men to be saved and to come to the knowledge of the truth." 1 Timothy 2:4* Their ordained names, displaying His name, Jesus. If we are desiring world revival, we must co-labor with Father in the lives of our children to bring full revival. *"Being fully assured that what God promised, He is able to perform." Romans 4:21*

The task of parenting such powerful world changers is huge! The responsibility is both a privilege and an honor that deserves our highest priority. The New Testament repeatedly attests to the importance of cultivating and upholding strong, wholesome families. Humanly, we are not perfect parents but we are perfected parents as we commune with Him; practicing forgiveness and repentance, allowing His Grace to become our strengths as we pour out the love of Christ to our children.[115]

The whole Bible is a Book about God the Father extravagantly loving His kids. At times, parenting or teaching children may not appear glamorous, but it is extremely glorious under the manifold Presence and love of God. Allow God to love you and love your children out of His love. Honor your child by pulling them in from the outskirts and into the heart of the Father, *for the Kingdom of Heaven belongs to such as these.*[116]

Take notice of each child that God has placed in your path. What do you recognize? What fruits of the Spirit are manifesting in their actions? What positive characteristics are making themselves known in big or subtle ways?

Strengthen them by calling out the gold that you see in them. Help them to think rightly about themselves. Encourage them as they are delighting in what they are doing. Find ways to help them express their God given desires, asking Holy Spirit how to position your child in this season. Should you contribute financially? Should you give of your time more? Should you position them for further training? Should you just sit back and watch them go? He will direct your steps and furthermore, direct His children's steps in the way they should go. Train them to look to Daddy God and recognize the different ways in which He responds. Can you imagine the tremendous impact a child will have on the world when he or she is attune to the Living God?

TOUCHING THE WORLD THROUGH YOU

Akiane, is a powerful example of the way the Lord wants to touch the world through your unique mark. At the age of four she began sketching. At age six, she started painting on canvases. Akiane was having dreams and encounters with God and she knew nothing of Him up to that point. Her family was unconvinced of religion but provided her the opportunity to explore her giftings. At age seven, Akiane lead her own family to the Lord; her giftings and encounters continuing to increase and excel. She has been brought before very influential people; her works draw people into heavenly encounters with the King of Kings.

God purposed each child for such a time as this. He purposed them with their own DNA so they might display His Divine Nature Assuredly.

God purposed each child for such a time as this. He purposed them with their own DNA so they might display His Divine Nature Assuredly in their realms of influence in their unique way. *"Blessed be the God and Father of our Lord Jesus Christ, who has blessed us with every spiritual blessing in the heavenly places in Christ, just as He chose us in Him before the foundation of the world, that we would be holy and blameless before Him. In love He predestined us to adoption as sons through Jesus Christ to Himself, according to the kind intention of His will, to the praise of the glory of His grace, which He freely bestowed on us in the Beloved. In Him we have redemption through His blood, the forgiveness of our trespasses, according to the riches of His grace which He lavished on us. In all wisdom and insight He made known to us the mystery of His will, according to His kind intention which He purposed in Him with a view to an administration suitable to the fullness of the*

times, that is, the summing up of all things in Christ, things in the heavens and things on the earth. In Him also we have obtained an inheritance, having been predestined according to His purpose who works all things after the counsel of His will, to the end that we who were the first to hope in Christ would be to the praise of His glory. In Him, you also, after listening to the message of truth, the gospel of your salvation— having also believed, you were sealed in Him with the Holy Spirit of promise, who is given as a pledge of our inheritance, with a view to the redemption of God's own possession, to the praise of His glory."
Ephesians 1:3-14

There may be parts of Heaven that are not fully experienced or released on earth unless every believer is courageously living in truth of their purpose. Even if you are not intentionally ministering to those around you; you are. You are *the Lady or Gentleman of the Lamp,* the light of His Marvelous Light, reflecting His glory. *"For so the Lord has commanded us, I have placed you as a light for the Gentiles, that you may bring salvation to the end of the earth."*
Acts 13:47

> *There may be parts of Heaven that are not fully experienced or released on earth unless every believer is courageously living the truth of their purpose.*

Throughout history, there have been babies and young children who have become King in their monarchy due to deaths and resignations in their royal line. There were people privileged and delegated among these young kings to keep charge over them, guiding them along as they reigned throughout the monarchy until they came of age.

You are privileged and delegated among your young kings and queens to keep charge over them, guiding them as they reign and mature in the Kingdom.[117] Even though they are not of age, great things can happen through them that will impact the world for His glory.[118] Some may be noticeably grand while other acts may seem small until further realized down the road. These young kings will become grand kings in their called fields of influence. Kingly children have the ability to release Heaven, making advances that no one before them has yet touched; all for the glory of King Jesus!

VICTORY DISPLAYED THROUGH A FULL BRIDE

These young kings will become grand kings in their called fields of influence.

Praise God for your love and pursuit of Him and your position to champion your children into what was purposefully intended for them. Do not look at this responsibility lightly for the restoration of the world to be made complete, originates with kingly children who will exercise their royal authority rightly. *"Creation itself also will be set free from its slavery to corruption into the freedom of the glory of the children of God." Romans 8:21* Guard what was committed to your trust, stewarding the reign of heaven in your children's lives.[119]

The current state of the world is in abundant need of an awakening to Truth through Love. Thank God for the Bride of Christ making herself ready, adorning herself in the gifts from Heaven to usher in the Bridegroom with a victorious Bride awaiting His arrival!

The majority of the Bride, for a time, seemed hidden away from the evil of the world in a cocoon. The church, closing herself off to the world around, trying to protect its culture, came to the realization that without light, darkness dwells. Now, the Bride, is awakening across the earth to let Christ's glory be boldly displayed through her; beautifying the world and transforming lives for the King of glory.

We are meant to demonstrate love through signs and wonders so the world might come into the splendor and knowledge of Him; eyewitnesses of His majesty. Christ, our Bridegroom, lavished His gifts upon us, without measure so that His Testimony may be fully revealed in Love.[120] We, the Bride of Christ, are beginning to align ourselves with Father's original design and move as one with Him. We are beginning to display His glory effortlessly to the world around us as we rise above all things, our power derived from the Son.[121]

This victorious, emerging Bride is already underway and will come into full, bursting transfiguration when children are readied in the group. A herd of butterflies is called a kaleidoscope. This term stunningly depicts the beautiful glory of the whole church displaying His manifested Light through the ones who uniquely reflect the very facets of His face; many colors revealed, streaming from the rainbow encompassing His Majestic throne room. We will soon see some of the greatest signs and wonders as the world comes into agreement with Heaven's rule as we let the children come. For such is the Kingdom of heaven and for such a time as this! Come Lord Jesus, come. We thank You and adore You! All glory and honor to Lord Jesus, Amen!

PONDER THE POSSIBILITIES

Start dreaming BIG with God and write them down. Now, know this, He will do even more than that!

Think of the ways God has worked powerfully through these children. How will God work powerfully through yours?

Are there really obstacles in your life or invitations into experiencing more of Heaven? Think of different areas that need Heaven to come crashing into. What do you have to give into it? God's Kingdom is NOW.

PROCLAIM

My young kids will become grand kings.

My children have the ability to release Heaven and make advances that no one before them has yet touched.

Great and marvelous things happen through me and my children.

Our DNA displays His Divine Nature Assuredly.

Raising up the children whom the Lord has given me are both a privilege and an honor.

I rule and reign with Jesus.

I carry the Light of the world. It transforms darkness to light.

I am born to change the world.

I will see some of the greatest signs and wonders.

BE FRUITFUL AND MULTIPLY

Spend time with Daddy God. Ask Him to show you how He has made your son and daughter unique and special to Him. Then, tell your child and continually remind him or her of who God says they are.

What does He love watching them do? What does He delight in with them? What gifts is He excitedly revealing to them?

Share all that Daddy God has to say about your child with him or her.

Have your children rest before the Lord and picture Jesus' face. Tell them that Jesus has a special place He likes to go with them and He is going to take them there. Tell them to take Jesus' hand and walk with Him there. After some time, ask them what they saw.

Tell them that Jesus wants to give them a special gift. Have your child open up his or hands before Jesus to receive it. What did they receive?

You can also, have them play before God and ask them how Jesus delights in them.

Always remind them of who they are and what they are destined for. All of creation is longing for the sons and daughters of God to be revealed!

CLOSING SCRIPTURAL PRAYER

"Therefore I also, after I heard of your faith in the Lord Jesus and your love for all the saints, do not cease to give thanks for you, making mention of you in my prayers: that the God of our Lord Jesus Christ, the Father of glory, may give to you the spirit of wisdom and revelation in the knowledge of Him, the eyes of your understanding being enlightened; that you may know what is the hope of His calling, what are the riches of the glory of His inheritance in the saints, and what is the exceeding greatness of His power toward us who believe, according to the working of His mighty power which He worked in Christ when He raised Him for the dead and seated Him in His right hand in the heavenly places, far above all principality and power and might and dominion, in every name that is named, not only in this age but also in that which is to come. And He put all these things under His feet, and gave Him to be head over all things to the church, which is His body, the fullness of Him who fills all in all."
Ephesians 1:15-23

ENDNOTES

Chapter 1:

1 | Matthew 10:8; 28:18-20
2 | Mark 16:20, Acts 4:29-30, 1 Peter 2:9-10, 2 Peter 1:3-4
3 | Matthew 13:11, Luke 8:10, John 1:16, 1 Corinthians 4:1, Ephesians 2:18; 3:12, Colossians 1:26
4 | John 17:23, 1 Corinthians 6:17, Galatians 2:20, 1 John 3:24
5 | Joshua 1:9, Matthew 28:20, Romans 8:11, 1 Corinthians 3:16
6 | Ephesians 1:20; 2:6
7 | Romans 8:34
8 | Psalm 91:11, Hebrews 1:7; 1:14
9 | Romans 5:17; 6:13, 2 Corinthians 5:21; 6:18, Galatians 3:26-29; 4:5-6, James 1:12, 1 Peter 5:4, 1 John 3:1
10 | Psalm 34:10; 36:8; 132:15, Philippians 4:19, 2 Corinthians 9:8, 2 Peter 1:10-12
11 | Psalm 5:12, Proverbs 8:35, John 1:16, Romans 14:17
12 | Psalm 17:8, Ephesians 3:20
13 | Luke 12:32
14 | John 5:21, Romans 4:17
15 | Acts 13:28-29, Romans 5:18; 6:4; 8:2-4

16| Romans 1:17, 2 Peter 1:2-4
17| John 14:12

Chapter 2:

18| Acts 13:32-34, Romans 8:16-18; 14:17
19| Matthew 11:25, Acts 10:34, 2 Corinthians 4:5-15,
1 Timothy 4:12
20| Job 9:10, Isaiah 55:9, Romans 5:2; 11:33,
Ephesians 2:18; 3:12
21| strephó G4762
22| Mark 1:15
23| Isaiah 41:10, Ephesians 2:4-10
24| Matthew 7:8; 21:22, John 14:13-14, 1 John 5:14-15,
2 Corinthians 3:5; 12:19
25| 2 Corinthians 12:9; 13:4
26| 2 Corinthians 3:5, Hebrews 12:2
27| Romans 8:37, Ephesians 3:16-19, 1 John 4:19
28| John 16:30, Colossians 2:2-4
29| Matthew 3:8, Mark 1:15
30| Romans 4:20-21
31| 2 Corinthians 4:7
32| Psalm 119:160, John 3:33-34, Colossians 1:5-6
33| John 14
34| Romans 5:17, 15:13, Ephesians 3:19
35| Luke 18:16, Acts 13:32-34
36| 2 Corinthians 9:10
37| Ephesians 1
38| Romans 8:19
39| Philippians 2:1-18
40| John 3:33-34, Philippians 1:6

Chapter 3:

41| Matthew 28:17-19, Luke 9:1; 10:1-23
42| mathētēs G3101

43| 2 Timothy 3:14, 2 Peter 3:17-18, Deuteronomy 6:7,
       Psalm 78:5; 132:12
44| Ephesians 1:13, 2 Corinthians 1:21-23, John 14:12
45| Philippians 2:1-8
46| 1 John 3:22
47| Philippians 2:12-13, John 16:23-27, Romans 8:24-30
48| Galatians 6:10, Colossians 4:5-6, 2 Timothy 4:2,
       Titus 3:1, 1 Peter 1:3-21
49| 1 Corinthians 1:4-9, Psalm 78:4
50| Matthew 25
51| 1 Corinthians 5:8, 1 Timothy 2:4
52| Acts 3:16; 4:30, John 15:5
53| Jeremiah 17:7, Proverbs 3:26, 2 Corinthians 3:4,
       Colossians 2:6, Hebrews 3:6; 4:16; 12:2, 1 John 5:14
54| Psalm 37:24; 145:14
55| Ephesians 1, Romans 8:28-30
56| 1 Corinthians 1:6, 2 Corinthians 4:7-12

Chapter 4:

57| Psalm 19:7; 25:10; 93:5; 119, John 3:33, 1 Kings 2:3
58| Psalm 119:24; 119:29; 119:167; 119:59, Romans 1:17,
       Colossians 3:4, 1 Thessalonians 2:13; 5:24
59| Psalm 119:111-112; 132:7-18, 2 Timothy 3:15
60| Psalm 119:144, 1 John 5:11
61| John 3:33
62| Joshua 1:9, Matthew 28:20, Revelation 19:10
63| 2 Corinthians 4:7-12
64| Romans 6:5, Galatians 6:14, Ephesians 2:16, 1 Peter
       2:24
65| Ephesians 2:17-19; 3:11-13, Romans 8:21, Galatians 5:1
66| John 14:12, 2 Corinthians 3, Ephesians 3:20
67| Romans 2:7; 8:21; 9:23, 2 Corinthians 1:20,
       Colossians 3:14, 1 Peter 4:14
68| John 5:20; 17:1-2, Colossians 3:4, James 1:23-25
69| Romans 5:2, Ephesians 4:15; 6:10-20, 2 Peter 3:18

70| pisteuō G4100
71| Deuteronomy 11:18-25, John 10:25; 15:27, 1 John 1:1-4
72| Habakkuk 2:2
73| Matthew 28:19-20, Acts 13:32-33, 2 Corinthians 3
74| Acts 2:39; 13:32-34, Romans 8:21, 1 John 4:4

Chapter 5:

75| Psalm 33:11; 78:5-7; 145:4
76| 2 Chronicles 5:13, Ezra 3:11, Psalm 18:3; 22:3; 40:3
77| John 11:40
78| Ephesians 1, Hebrews 12:1-3
79| chagag H2287
80| Romans 1:21; 8:1, 2 Corinthians 3; 4:15
81| Exodus 23:16; 34:22
82| 2 Corinthians 9:10-12, Philippians 4, Romans 15:10,
1 Thessalonians 5:9-24
83| Chronicles 16:8, Psalm 97:12; 116:17,
Colossians 3:17, Romans 1:21, Acts 11:23
84| 1 Corinthians 13:12, 2 Corinthians 4, Colossians 2:6-7,
James 2:22
85| Ephesians 3:10, Luke 8:15
86| Romans 10:17, Philippians 4
87| Acts 2, Philippians 4:19, Titus 3:5-7
88| John 3:34, Colossians 2:2-3, 1 Thessalonians 5:11,
1 Peter 1:2, Hebrews 3:13
89| Hebrews 12:1-2, John 17:26
90| John 17:26, 1 Timothy 6:12
91| 1 Corinthians 16:13, Ephesians 6:10, 2 Timothy 2:1
92| Colossians 1:13, 2 Peter 1:11
93| Acts 13:22
94| emeth H571
95| Philippians 4:19, Romans 15:15, Hebrews 10:23
96| Romans 9:23, John 17:10, Acts 9:15, Acts 9:28
97| 1 Corinthians 3:11
98| Acts 17:28, Ephesians 5:1-2, 1 John 14

99| Haggai 2:7, Romans 8:19
100| Isaiah 29:22-24, 1 John 3-5, 2 John 1:1-3
101| Isaiah 62:3, 2 Corinthians 5:4-6, Ephesians 1:3-4; 1:11;
   2:10, Colossians 1:17, 2 Corinthians 5:4-6
102| Matthew 10:8, 1 Corinthians 2:12
103| Galatians 3:26, Romans 8:15-18
104| Ephesians 3
105| Psalm 11:7; 17:15, 2 Corinthians 3:18; 4:6;
   1 Corinthians 1:4-9
106| 1 Peter 2:5
107| 1 Corinthians 15:57, 1 John 5:4, Revelation 17:14,
   2 Corinthians 10:3-5
108| 1 Thessalonians 4:1, Colossians 2:2-3
109| 1 Peter 2:9, Romans 10:15
110| Isaiah 61:1, 2 Corinthians 4:13-15
111| Proverbs 16:23, Romans 10:8-10
112| Philippians 2:15, 1 John 4:4, Revelation 5:9-11
   Psalm 69:35
113| Galatians 3:8, Philippians 2:18, Hebrews 2:13-15
114| Ephesians 1:6-8, Acts 9:15, 1 John 4:4
115| John 17:23, Romans 12:23, 2 Corinthians 2:19,
   Philippians 1:6
116| Matthew 1:14
117| 1 Peter 5:2-4, Galatians 4:2
118| Acts 9:15, 1 Timothy 4:12-16, John 17:5
119| Proverbs 22:6, 2 Timothy 1:14, 2 John 1:1-3,
   1 Peter 4:10
120| 1 Corinthians
121| Ephesians 3:10-12

APPENDIX

Figures 1-4: Real - time sonography and multiplanar sonographic images obtained on a Siemens Antares ultrasound unit on 7/22/2016. US Transvaginal (Pregnant)

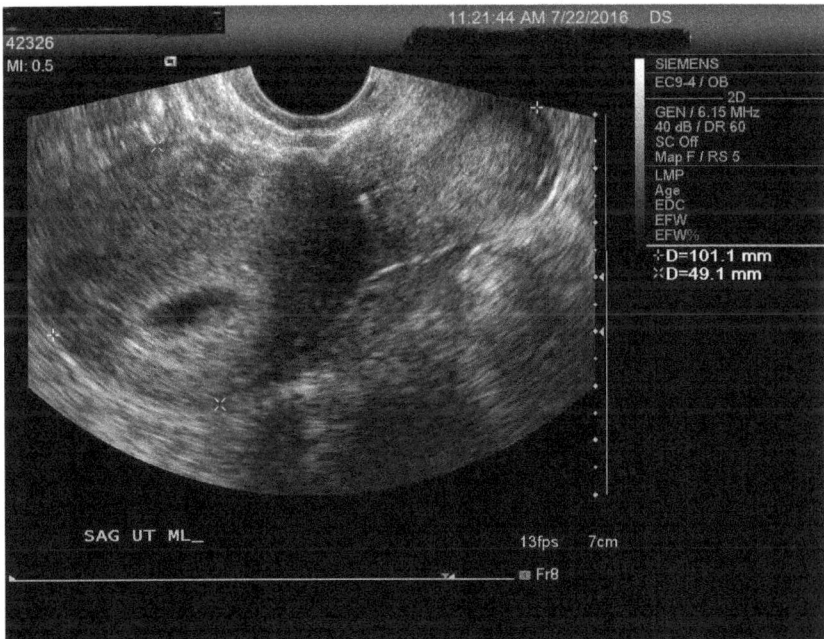

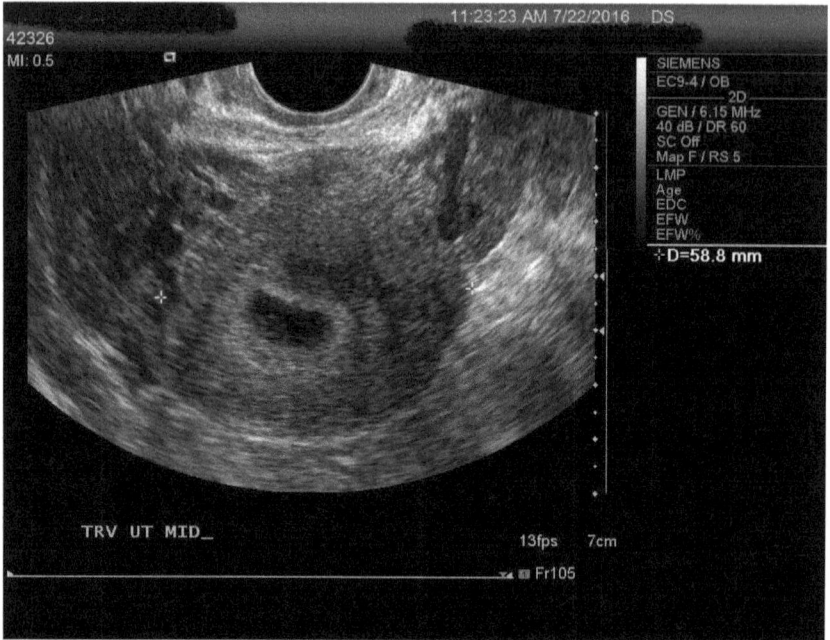

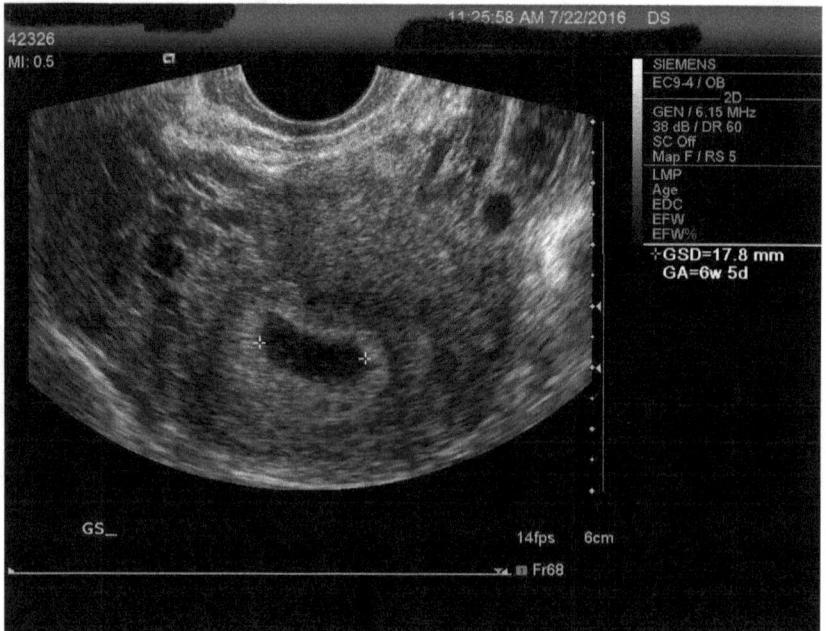

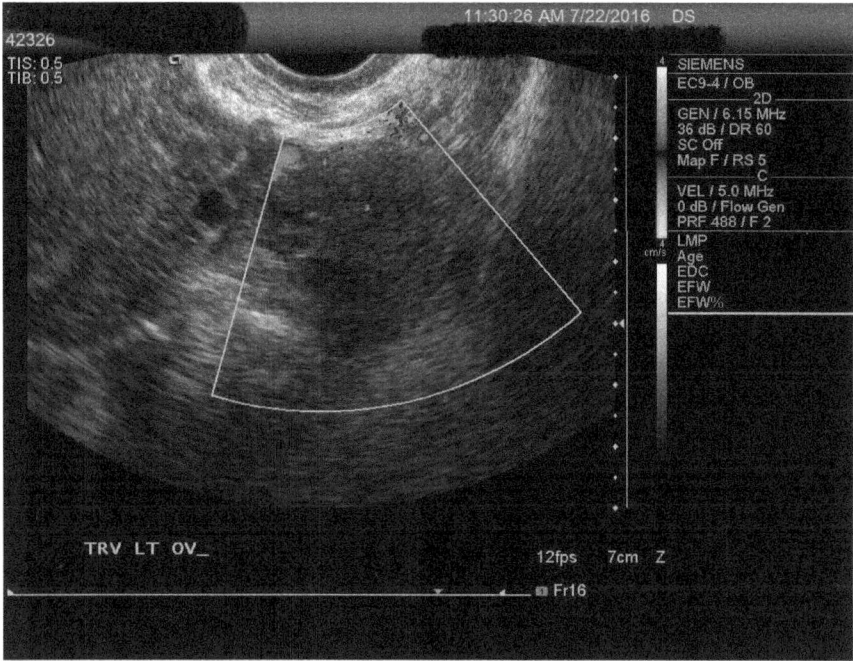

Figure 5 - First OBGYN "Good News" appointment
consultation post lifeless ultrasound scans and bloodwork.

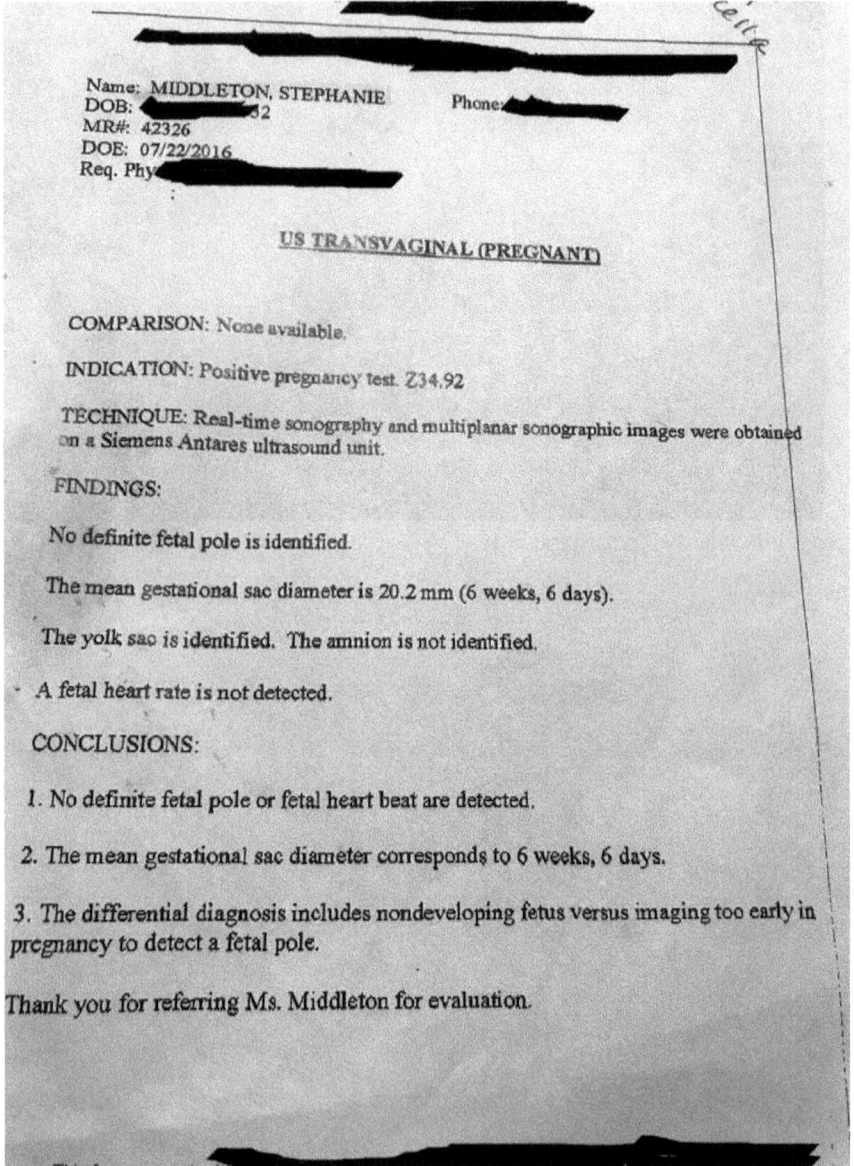

Name: MIDDLETON, STEPHANIE
DOB: ⬛⬛⬛⬛62   Phone:⬛⬛⬛⬛
MR#: 42326
DOE: 07/22/2016
Req. Phy⬛⬛⬛⬛

US TRANSVAGINAL (PREGNANT)

COMPARISON: None available.

INDICATION: Positive pregnancy test. Z34.92

TECHNIQUE: Real-time sonography and multiplanar sonographic images were obtained on a Siemens Antares ultrasound unit.

FINDINGS:

No definite fetal pole is identified.

The mean gestational sac diameter is 20.2 mm (6 weeks, 6 days).

The yolk sac is identified. The amnion is not identified.

A fetal heart rate is not detected.

CONCLUSIONS:

1. No definite fetal pole or fetal heart beat are detected.

2. The mean gestational sac diameter corresponds to 6 weeks, 6 days.

3. The differential diagnosis includes nondeveloping fetus versus imaging too early in pregnancy to detect a fetal pole.

Thank you for referring Ms. Middleton for evaluation.

Figure 6: Return OBGYN visit report of miraculous turn of events – "Good News" revealed!

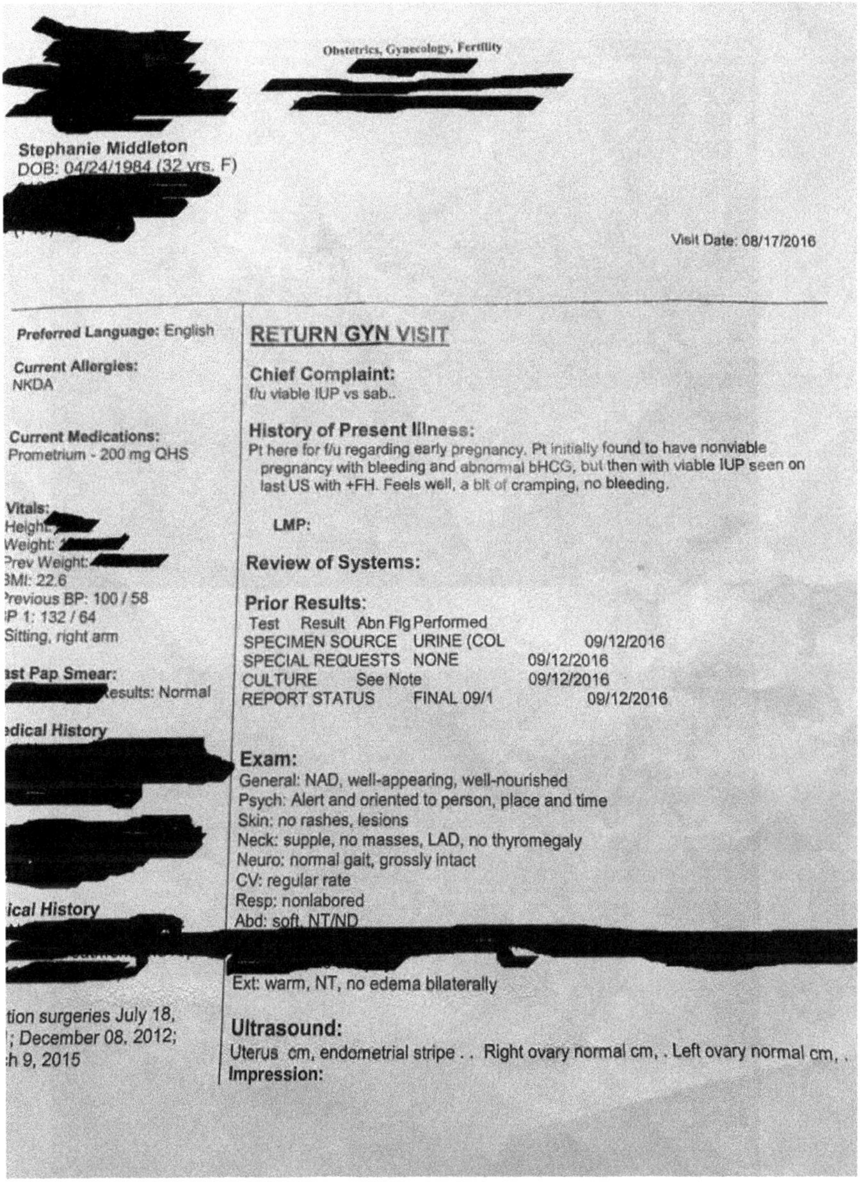

Obstetrics, Gynecology, Fertility

Stephanie Middleton
DOB: 04/24/1984 (32 yrs. F)

Visit Date: 08/17/2016

Preferred Language: English

Current Allergies:
NKDA

Current Medications:
Prometrium - 200 mg QHS

Vitals:
Height:
Weight:
Prev Weight:
BMI: 22.6
Previous BP: 100 / 58
BP 1: 132 / 64
Sitting, right arm

Last Pap Smear:
Results: Normal

Medical History

ical History

tion surgeries July 18,
; December 08, 2012;
h 9, 2015

RETURN GYN VISIT

Chief Complaint:
f/u viable IUP vs sab..

History of Present Illness:
Pt here for f/u regarding early pregnancy. Pt initially found to have nonviable pregnancy with bleeding and abnormal bHCG, but then with viable IUP seen on last US with +FH. Feels well, a bit of cramping, no bleeding.

LMP:

Review of Systems:

Prior Results:
Test   Result Abn Flg Performed
SPECIMEN SOURCE   URINE (COL   09/12/2016
SPECIAL REQUESTS   NONE   09/12/2016
CULTURE   See Note   09/12/2016
REPORT STATUS   FINAL 09/1   09/12/2016

Exam:
General: NAD, well-appearing, well-nourished
Psych: Alert and oriented to person, place and time
Skin: no rashes, lesions
Neck: supple, no masses, LAD, no thyromegaly
Neuro: normal gait, grossly intact
CV: regular rate
Resp: nonlabored
Abd: soft, NT/ND

Ext: warm, NT, no edema bilaterally

Ultrasound:
Uterus cm, endometrial stripe .. Right ovary normal cm, . Left ovary normal cm, .
Impression:

Figures 7-8: Ultrasound images of a healthy baby girl with a good heartbeat developing in the womb.

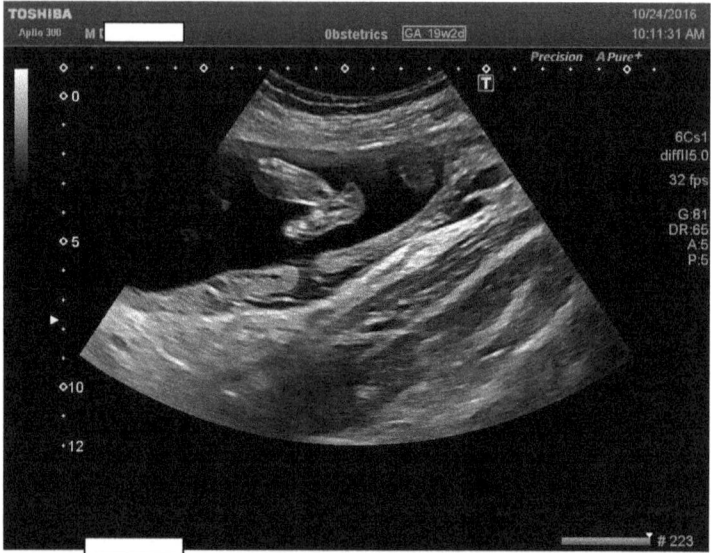

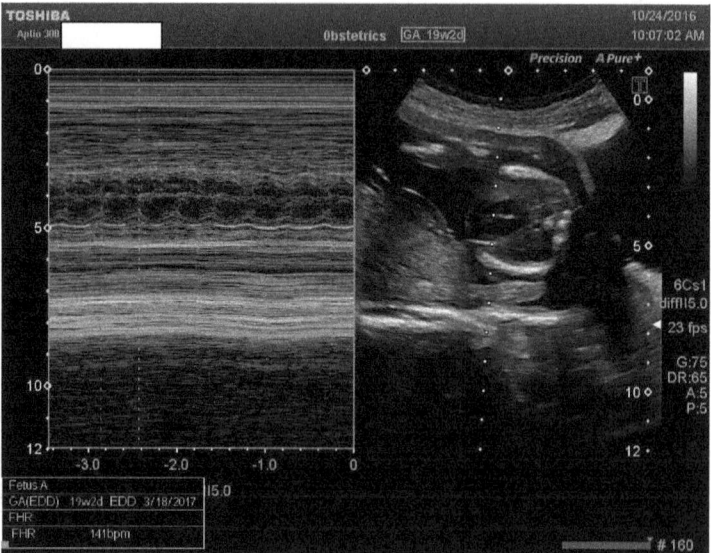

Figures 9-10 Photos of Emma post healthy delivery. Pictured below, newborn Emma

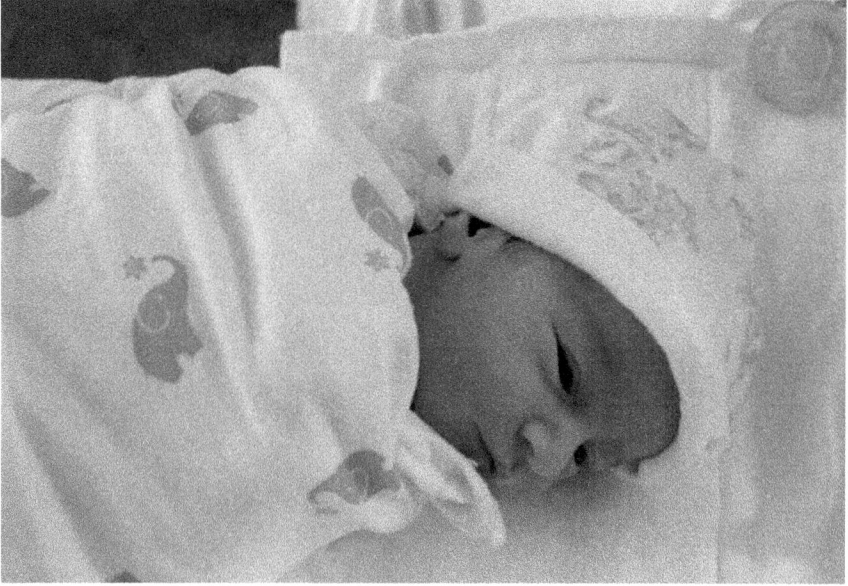

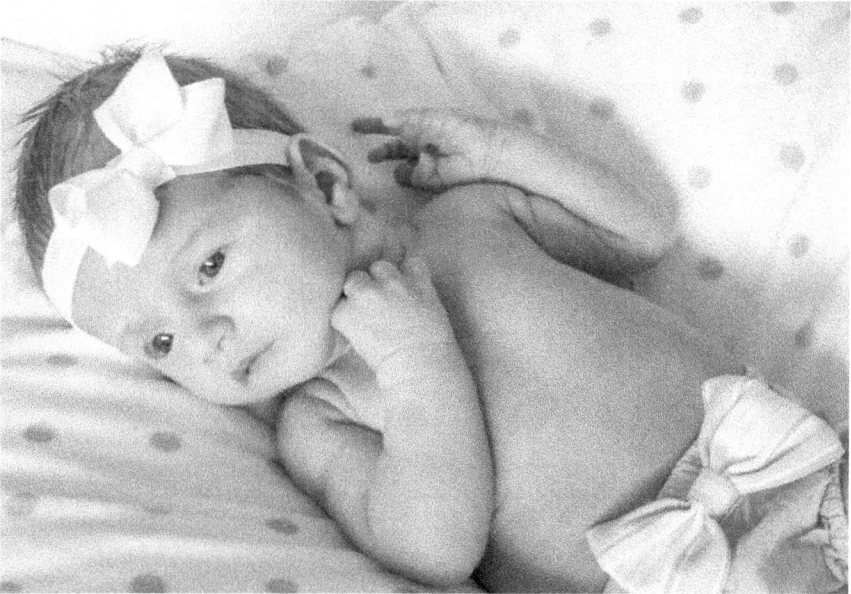

Figures 11-12 Photos of our four children: Tyler, Emma, Cailyn, Noah

www.ingramcontent.com/pod-product-compliance
Lightning Source LLC
Chambersburg PA
CBHW051831090426
42736CB00011B/1749

9 780692 955284